PRETTY

TOUGH

PLANTS

PRETTY TOUGH PLANTS

135 Resilient, Water-Smart Choices for a Beautiful Garden

BY THE EXPERTS AT **PLANT SELECT**

TIMBER PRESS
Portland, Oregon

CONTENTS

INTRODUCTION

Fifty years ago, gardens across much of America looked conspicuously the same: bluegrass lawns, a foundation planting of junipers (or yews perhaps) with a fringe of annuals planted between the green monocultures. But with the birth of xeriscaping and a pride in distinctive regional landscapes, the face of the American garden began rapidly changing, and the "perennial boom" of the early 1980s has morphed into a "perennial celebration" for many gardeners, further transforming landscapes and gardens across the country. In the Rocky Mountain west, Plant Select spearheaded the movement in the 1990s by providing a rich palette of native and adapted trees, shrubs, perennials, and even a few annuals which thrive in the changeable climate locals enjoy and sometimes complain about.

WHAT IS PLANT SELECT?

Plant Select is the country's leading brand of plants designed to thrive in high plains and intermountain regions, offering plants that provide more beauty with less work so gardeners of all levels can achieve smart, stunning, and successful gardens using fewer resources and with a more positive environmental impact.

Driven by the belief that the right plants in the right place matter and that cultivating plants in tougher growing environments requires smarter approaches, Plant Select leverages a uniquely collaborative model and highly selec-

◀ A stunning xeriscape at Kendrick Lake Gardens in Lakewood, Colorado, proves that water-thrifty gardening can be beautiful.

▲ An excellent source of nectar, *Salvia darcyi* 'Pscarl' (VERMILION BLUFFS Mexican sage) attracts hummingbirds with it large red, tube-shaped flowers.

Funding is provided through grants, memberships, and royalties. Each plant is assigned a royalty fee, and licensed growers remit fees based on sales, and the use of the Plant Select brand is only available to licensed growers. Plants in the program fall into two categories: recommended and introduced. Recommended plants are already available in the trade but are little known or underused. Introductions are plants that are new to horticulture, and are often patented or named with registered trademarks.

Since the flagship promotion in 1997, 140 regular selections and 12 petites (well-adapted, smaller plants that have not yet been readily available to gardeners) have been featured through 2016. This book describes all of these plants in celebration of the program's twentieth anniversary.

WHAT DOES IT TAKE TO BECOME A PLANT SELECT PLANT?

Since Plant Select was first conceived there has been great impetus on promoting plants that fit a rigorous set of qualities. Every plant is evaluated on these seven points:

- ▸ Thrives in a broad range of conditions
- ▸ Flourishes with less water
- ▸ Resilience in challenging climates
- ▸ Uniqueness/one of a kind
- ▸ Disease and insect resistance
- ▸ Long-lasting beauty
- ▸ Non-invasiveness

Refined over the years, this list of features is the guiding rule before any plant can move forward through the program and ultimately to the horticultural trade and gardening public.

New plants come to Plant Select through a variety of avenues. Some are selections found in nature, some are developed by breeders, some are discovered by nursery professionals, and others are from collections at DBG or selections made through trials. When a plant is suggested, a committee of growers makes a decision to move forward with the plant (or not) based on the seven-point system above.

Plant Select has developed an intensive trial program with DBG and CSU. Every new plant under consideration is grown at both locations and evaluated on garden performance in field trials through at least two winters. While in field trials, a portion of the plants is allowed to go to seed to evaluate for potential invasiveness. If seedlings or runners are produced to an undesirable extent the plant is removed from consideration. Annual summer evaluations are undertaken by a committee at both the CSU and DBG sites. Using the seven-point system, committee members score each plant. These scores are combined with empirical data recorded bi-weekly, and compiled into databases to help with the final selection process.

Once a plant has been through the trialing process and is considered for Plant Select promotions, the work of building up stock for production takes place. The entire process from inception to release can take between five and twenty years. All this effort is worth making sure that only the most qualified plants carry the Plant Select name.

WHY THIS MATTERS

Plant Select plays an increasingly important role for home gardeners from the novice to the experienced, as well as for landscape and nursery professionals. The primary focus of Plant Select is for the high-altitude Rocky Mountain region, although the information and palette of plants are appropriate for regions beyond. As the gardening public becomes more educated and discerning when selecting plants for gardens, there's a growing demand for plants that not only look attractive in the landscape but require less maintenance and less water, and are dependably hardy in a wide range of conditions. Plant Select plants serve these criteria well.

Anyone with an interest in gardening and sourcing plants that thrive in challenging situations will benefit from the information here. In addition, the photography provides proof of the beauty and diversity of the Plant Select portfolio and serves to inspire creative settings for amateur and professional gardeners alike. Successful gardening begins with planting the right plants in the right places and Plant Select makes gardening easier by showing how to plant smarter.

▲ Native prairie zinnia is a source of both pollen and nectar for a wild variety of pollinators, including native blue butterflies.

HOW TO USE THIS BOOK

This publication provides a comprehensive overview of plants in the Plant Select program that are available commercially and have proven hardy and noninvasive in the landscape. Each description is illustrated and includes specific details regarding mature plant size, season of bloom, and the plant's best features, along with cultural needs (including best methods of propagation), landscape features and design ideas, as well the native range and origin of the plant. A chart at the end of the book can be used to find a plant for a particular purpose or spot in the garden or landscape.

TYPES OF PLANTS

The plant descriptions are separated into groups by type of plant:

▸ **Tender perennials and annuals** Long-blooming plants that are adapted to warmer climates, but may overwinter in protected spots in colder areas

▸ **Petites** Lesser-known, smaller-statured, hardy plants that are good for rock gardens and small spaces

▸ **Groundcovers** Low-growing, spreading plants that come back every year

▸ **Perennials** Herbaceous plants that come back every year, but often die to the ground during winter

▸ **Grasses** Annual and perennial ornamental grasses

▸ **Vines** Annual and perennial vines

▸ **Shrubs** Woody plants that need little care

▸ **Trees and conifers** Smaller, ornamental trees and evergreen conifers

GENERAL CULTURAL INFORMATION

Many of the plants described in this book prefer well-drained soils so it's often advisable to add sand and/or smaller-grained gravel to slow-draining soils such as those heavy in clay particles. Building raised or mounded planting beds is an option, making it easier to create the most desirable soil structure. Gravel mulches are superior to wood or bark mulches for these native and adapted plants because mineral mulches are stable and don't break down, adding unwanted extra organic matter to the soil.

If a plant's hardiness is in question, place it closer to a building or large rocks, which will create a warmer microclimate for more protection. South sides of buildings are warmer than open areas, as well.

Keep newly planted plants well-watered but not saturated. Taper off the water as the plant appears able to maintain health and growth with less frequent irrigation. It may take a year or more for perennials to become established, and two or more years for shrubs, trees, and conifers. Winter watering, especially in dry climates, is advised during warm spells with no snow cover. Xeric plants should be watered until fully established, and then will survive on natural precipitation under most conditions.

Most of the plants in this book grow well with only light applications of balanced organic or natural fertilizer to restore soil health and fertility, and to keep growth moderate; high nitrogen chemical fertilizers may cause weak, leggy growth. Fertilizer application is usually performed in the spring when new growth is vigorously emerging and elongating.

Pruning, cutting back, and other maintenance tasks are individually specific; see "Tips from the Pros" for each plant at www.plantselect.org for details.

PLANT PROFILE TERMS DEFINED

Size
Estimated height and width of the plant at maturity

Soils
▸ **Clay** Fine-grained soil type that holds water longer and is slower-draining than other soil types

▸ **Loam** Moderately drained soil type containing some organic content

▸ **Sandy** Coarse-grained, mineral soil types that drain quickly and don't retain water well

▸ **Well-drained** Water moves through the soil reasonably quickly and doesn't stand and pool; puddles last less than an hour or two

Hardiness Zones
The USDA hardiness zone rating system is based on average *minimum temperatures*. Lower zone rated plants are more cold hardy.

Zone 3	to -40°F
Zone 4	to -30°F
Zone 5	to -20°F
Zone 6	to -10°F
Zone 7	to 0°F
Zone 8	to 10°F
Zone 9	to 20°F
Zone 10	to 30°F

http://planthardiness.ars.USDA.gov/PHZMWeb/

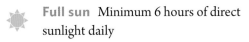

UNDERSTANDING ICONS

Full sun Minimum 6 hours of direct sunlight daily

Partial sun/partial shade Needs 3–4 hours of direct sunlight daily

Shade Requires little to no direct sunlight daily

Moderate Water regularly through the season

Dry Provide extra water only when dry

Xeric Little to no additional irrigation once established

Pollinators Attracts bees, butterflies, and/or hummingbirds. May also be host plant for caterpillars.

Deer resistant Infrequently browsed by deer

TENDER PERENNIALS AND ANNUALS

Gazania krebsiana

TANAGER gazania • Asteraceae (aster family)

SIZE ▸ 2–3 in. tall, 6–10 in. wide

FLOWERS ▸ orange, early spring through fall

BEST FEATURES ▸ bright orange-yellow flowers over attractive evergreen rosettes; long-blooming; very drought tolerant

TANAGER is a highly uniform strain of South African *Gazania krebsiana*, which typically has red-orange flowers. TANAGER, however, has large (3-inch) yellow-orange flowers with a dark eye. The plant withstands spring frost as well as intense summer heat and drought, and the glossy green foliage acquires a purplish hue in winter.

CULTURE

Full sun to partial shade. Clay, loam, or sandy soil. Moderate watering to xeric. Plants tolerate spring frost and can be put out in the garden in early spring, even coming out of a greenhouse. In some gardens an abundance of seedlings may be produced; these are easily transplanted or removed. Allowing plants to self-sow often creates a virtual long-blooming groundcover of many plants growing thickly together. Propagate by seeds, which germinate well after a 14- to 30-day cold stratification; do not cover seeds as they need light to germinate. USDA hardiness zones 6–9.

LANDSCAPE USE

TANAGER gazania is a wonderful addition to the xeriscape, sunny rock garden, or the edge of a dry border. Plants begin blooming very early in the spring and often continue through most of the summer into fall. The light orange flowers combine well with LITTLE TRUDY catmint, PLATINUM sage, VALLEY LAVENDER plains verbena, or CRYSTAL RIVER veronica. Attracts bees, butterflies, and moths.

NATIVE RANGE AND ORIGIN

The species is widespread and variable throughout the steppes of South Africa (the Karoo). The highly uniform strain TANAGER was selected by Kees Sahin, a great seedsman from the Netherlands, who authorized Plant Select to name it after the vivid American songbird which flashes the same brilliant orange shade.

Plectranthus argentatus

Silver dollar plant • Lamiaceae (mint family)

SIZE ▶ 20–36 in. tall, 20–40 in. wide

FLOWERS ▶ very small, white, on spikes, summer

BEST FEATURES ▶ felty, silvery green foliage; tolerates neglect and drought with flair; very attractive in containers throughout the growing season

One of the few annuals recommended by Plant Select, this shrubby Australian mint is perennial where frost does not occur. It is used primarily for its foliage. The species' name refers to the color of the abundant silvery recurved hairs on the leaves and young stems.

CULTURE

Full sun to partial shade. Loam. Moderate watering to dry. Remove flowers if desired to encourage more lush foliage growth. The plant is best started fresh each spring. Propagate by cuttings, which root easily. Some seed strains are available, but the Plant Select selection is grown from cuttings. USDA hardiness zones 10b–11, annual elsewhere in climates with frost.

LANDSCAPE USE

Silver dollar plant is excellent as an accent or massed in containers, annual plantings, or borders. This densely branched plant forms a medium-sized mound which looks lovely spilling over the sides of large containers. The narrow stalks of bluish white flowers are not very showy but add interest late in the season. Use as a filler plant among perennials such as Sonoran Sunset hyssop, CORAL CANYON twinspur, or Wild Thing and Furman's Red autumn sages. For a fabulous annual container planting, combine it with colorful calibrachoa, osteospermum, salvia, and an annual variegated grass. It also combines well with coleus. Attracts bees.

NATIVE RANGE AND ORIGIN

Silver dollar plant is native to north-central New South Wales and along the border with Queensland, Australia. Original germplasm for this form of the species was acquired by Rick Darke at Titoki Point Garden and Nursery on the North Island of Australia and introduced through Longwood Gardens' (Kennett Square, Pennsylvania) plant introduction program.

Rudbeckia 'Denver Daisy'

Denver Daisy black-eyed Susan • Asteraceae (aster family)

SIZE ▶ 18–28 in. tall, 10–25 in. wide

FLOWERS ▶ yellow with a dark eye ring, summer through fall

BEST FEATURES ▶ large yellow daisies with dark-lined centers; long season of showy bloom

Rudbeckia hirta (black-eyed Susan) brightens roadsides from the Rockies to the Appalachians and has been a cherished garden plant around the world for over two centuries. In recent decades, a wide spectrum of selections has been made for height, flower form, and habit. This flamboyant hybrid is deemed by many gardeners to be the most spectacular.

CULTURE

Full sun. Clay or loam; performs best in good garden soil. Moderate watering to dry; grows best with moderate irrigation during the hot and dry times of summer. Although it can occasionally come back and bloom a second year, it is best treated as an annual. Self-sown seed does not always come true to type. Propagate by commercial seed sources that breed true, or as plants purchased and planted in late spring. USDA hardiness zones 6–9.

LANDSCAPE USE

Denver Daisy is easily grown in a variety of soils and exposures provided it's not given too much shade. In containers, the showy blooms and compact, sturdy plants create a vivid show in late-summer and fall-themed combinations. Ornamental grasses such as Korean feather reed grass, Blonde Ambition blue grama grass, or WINDWALKER big bluestem combine well with Denver Daisy. It also pairs wonderfully with Ruby Moon hyacinth bean and winecups. Attracts bees, butterflies, and moths. Deer resistant.

NATIVE RANGE AND ORIGIN

The parent species, *Rudbeckia hirta*, is native to the Rocky Mountains and midwestern prairies. When introduced by Plant Select in 2009, this hybrid from Benary Seed was a fitting sesquicentennial tribute to the founding of Denver.

Scutellaria suffrutescens

Cherry skullcap • Lamiaceae (mint family)

SIZE ▶ 3–8 in. tall, 10–15 in. wide

FLOWERS ▶ red, spring through fall

BEST FEATURES ▶ tidy growth habit; continuous display of cherry-red flowers

Even outside of its hardiness zone, it is worthwhile to grow cherry skullcap in containers or as an annual for its carpet of red snapdragon-like flowers. The generic name *Scutellaria* is derived from the Latin *scutella* ("small dish"), referring to the bowl-shaped calyx which remains after the flowers drop. The specific name indicates that this species has a persistent woody base.

CULTURE

Full sun to partial shade. Loam, sandy soil, or amended clay. Moderate watering to dry. An occasional light shearing encourages a greater number of buds and blooms. Cut plants back to the ground in early spring. Propagate by seeds, which germinate well without pretreatment; cover seeds lightly and maintain uniform moisture until seedlings are established. Terminal stem cuttings treated with a rooting hormone root easily under intermittent mist. USDA hardiness zones 6–9 and protected sites in zone 5.

LANDSCAPE USE

Use in the front of a perennial border, in rock gardens, or in raised beds. Plants are more likely to overwinter in colder climates if placed next to a large rock or building. Cherry skullcap looks best when combined with other diminutive plants such as dwarf beach-head iris, Goldhill golden-aster, or dwarf piñon pine. Attracts bees, butterflies, and hummingbirds.

NATIVE RANGE AND ORIGIN

The species is native to northern Mexico and possibly southern Texas. The original germplasm for this plant was collected in Nuevo León, Mexico, and provided to Plant Select by Bluebird Nursery of Clarkson, Nebraska.

Androsace sarmentosa 'Chumbyi'

Silky rock jasmine • Primulaceae (primrose family)

SIZE ▶ 2–4 in. tall, 8–12 in. wide

FLOWERS ▶ pink, early summer

BEST FEATURES ▶ bright pink flowers with a yellow center; evergreen fuzzy rosettes

---

A long-time favorite of rock gardeners in Colorado, this selection has persisted and thrived in gardens for more than 30 years, and one planting was found still alive in an unattended rock garden in Colorado at 9400 ft. elevation after 12 years. Silky rock jasmine is very resilient; its rosettes can shrink down to a quarter of an inch when stressed and then expand again when water and care return.

CULTURE

Partial sun to shade. Loam, sandy soil, or amended clay. Moderate watering to dry. Plant is slow to establish but fills areas quickly after the second year. For more robust growth provide extra water and some light fertilization. Propagate by rosettes, which root easily in mid- to late summer. USDA hardiness zones 3–8.

LANDSCAPE USE

A very useful groundcover, the fuzzy rosettes provide year-round interest and the cheery pink flowers with yellow eyes cover the plant in early summer. It makes an excellent groundcover for dry shade, rock gardens, and under trees. For a beautiful early summer combination in partial sun, plant with dwarf beach-head iris and desert moss. Attracts bees.

NATIVE RANGE AND ORIGIN

Androsace sarmentosa is native to the Himalayas. The selection 'Chumbyi' was first propagated commercially by Marty Jones of Colorado Alpines in Vail, Colorado, in the 1980s.

Arenaria 'Wallowa Mountains'

Wallowa Mountains desert moss • Caryophyllaceae (pink family)

SIZE ▶ ½ in. tall, 8–12 in. wide

FLOWERS ▶ inconspicuous, white, spring

BEST FEATURES ▶ bright green cushion year-round; wonderful texture; xeric

For water-wise gardeners, the bright green, tight-growing foliage is a welcome contrast in color and form grown for its cushion-forming mats of green.

CULTURE

Full sun to partial shade. Well-drained loam or sandy soil. Moderate watering to xeric. Very low maintenance if cultural conditions are met. Propagate by cuttings or divisions. USDA hardiness zones 4–8.

LANDSCAPE USE

Desert moss is a useful and attractive plant for troughs, rock gardens, and fairy gardens, between paving stones, or as a contrast in xeric gardens with hardy cacti and succulents. It makes an excellent green roof plant in partial shade. It also tolerates the heat and humidity of the Midwest and Eastern United States. Gardeners in western states or in drier areas should consider desert moss as a true moss alternative, particularly in Japanese-style gardens or other small areas where the look of turf grass can be mimicked. Goldhill golden-aster, Scott's sugarbowls, low-growing sedums, and ice plants all make good pairings for desert moss. Attracts bees. Deer resistant.

NATIVE RANGE AND ORIGIN

Boyd Kline discovered this plant in the Wallowa Mountains of Oregon and Washington. It was introduced by Siskiyou Rare Plant Nursery, originally as a form of *Silene acaulis*, but upon flowering was determined to belong in the genus *Arenaria*.

Clematis scottii

Scott's sugarbowls • Ranunculaceae (buttercup family)

SIZE ▶ 12 in. tall, 15 in. wide

FLOWERS ▶ blue, late spring and early summer

BEST FEATURES ▶ nodding turban-shaped blue flowers; feathery seed heads; long-lived nonvining clumps

This native nonvining clematis is closely related to the more common *Clematis hirsutissima* (sugarbowls), but is smaller and continues to bloom into the summer months long after the regular sugarbowls have stopped. Blooms are followed by fuzzy feathery seed heads that are very ornamental as well.

CULTURE
Full sun. Loam, sandy, or amended clay soils. Moderate watering to xeric; avoid overwatering to keep plants compact. Deadhead if reblooming is desired. Alternatively, leave the showy seed heads on for midsummer interest. Cut the foliage back to the ground in late fall. Propagate by seeds, which need a warm stratification period followed by a cold stratification period; for best results plant seeds in early fall for spring germination. USDA hardiness zones 4–7.

LANDSCAPE USE
Scott's sugarbowls is perfect in a raised bed, rock garden, or large container. It grows especially well planted in full sun among rocks. Use it with other western native plants, including dwarf piñon pine, Blue Jazz single-leaf piñon pine, and dwarf forms of western columbines. Attracts bees, especially bumble bees. Deer resistant.

NATIVE RANGE AND ORIGIN
The species is native to mountainous parts of northern New Mexico and southern Colorado as far north as Colorado Springs. Kirk Fieseler of Laporte Avenue Nursery, Fort Collins, Colorado, first grew this particular form from seed collected in New Mexico in the late 1990s.

Draba rigida

Yellow stardust draba • Brassicaceae (mustard family)

SIZE ▶ 2–3 in. tall, 6–10 in. wide

FLOWERS ▶ yellow, spring

BEST FEATURES ▶ bright yellow flowers; green cushions of foliage

Few alpinelike plants can match this plant in its simplicity of form, with hummocks of tiny rosettes of bright green foliage and clear yellow flowers daintily hovering in the breeze hoping to lure bees and small insects to visit and pollinate it. Slow-growing but long-lived, this little draba is a true charmer to those willing to provide a smaller habitat to best appreciate its special qualities. This gem of a plant is truly petite.

CULTURE

Full sun to partial shade. Well-drained loam, sandy, or amended clay soil. Moderate watering to xeric. Low maintenance. Isolate this small plant from more vigorous growing plants. Propagate by division after flowering. USDA hardiness zones 4–8.

LANDSCAPE USE

Plant in outdoor containers or rock and fairy gardens where it won't be overgrown by more competitive plants. Locate it in an easily observable site, close to the edge of the rock or container garden so it can be best appreciated. Expect swarms of small yellow flowers over tight green buns of foliage in early spring. It combines well with dwarf beach-head iris, dwarf piñon pine, and desert moss. Attracts bees and small insects.

NATIVE RANGE AND ORIGIN

Yellow stardust draba is native to mountains of Turkey and Armenia.

Geranium dalmaticum

Dalmatian pink cranesbill • Geraniaceae (geranium family)

SIZE ▶ 6–8 in. tall and wide

FLOWERS ▶ pink, spring

BEST FEATURES ▶ showy pink flowers in spring and dark red foliage in fall

The foliage turns a bright red in fall and lasts several months. The foliage also has a nice fragrance making it less palatable to deer and rabbits. Though it's been available sporadically in horticulture, its durability and long season of interest make it worthy of being recognized through Plant Select.

CULTURE

Full sun to partial shade. Clay, loam, or sandy soil. Moderate watering to dry. Very tolerant of a wide range of soil types and sun exposures but thrives in free-draining soil that gets some supplemental irrigation. Requires very little regular maintenance. As plants get older areas can get slightly woody and open; cut out some of the oldest stems to encourage new growth. Propagate by cuttings. USDA hardiness zones 5–8.

LANDSCAPE USE

Dalmatian pink cranesbill is wonderful in the rock garden, perennial border, or at the front of the border in the cottage garden. It combines nicely with dwarf beach-head iris, dwarf piñon pine, desert moss, and most of the other Plant Select Petites. Attracts bees. Deer resistant.

NATIVE RANGE AND ORIGIN

This species is native to the Balkan Mountains of south-eastern Europe.

Heterotheca 'Goldhill'

Goldhill golden-aster • Asteraceae (aster family)

SIZE ▶ 1–2 in. tall, 5–10 in. wide

FLOWERS ▶ yellow, spring through fall

BEST FEATURES ▶ small yellow daisylike flowers; long-blooming; low maintenance; xeric

As a hybrid, Goldhill shows a wonderful vigor with a long season of bloom. The tidy little mounds of gray fuzzy foliage and its value to pollinators make this a great addition to a wide range of garden vignettes. In two-year trials at Colorado State University and Denver Botanic Gardens, Goldhill golden-aster was one of the top performers both years.

CULTURE
Full sun. Well-drained loam or sandy soil. Dry to xeric. Mostly maintenance free. Reblooms freely without deadheading. Propagate from cuttings, which will root fairly easily but care must be taken to not let moisture stay on the leaves too long or plants may rot. USDA hardiness zones 5–8.

LANDSCAPE USE
This plant is excellent for the rock garden, crevice garden, or trough and is best used as a focal point or an accent plant. Plants will even do well in spaces of stone patios or tucked into dry-stacked walls. It combines well with the smallest Plant Select Petites, including dwarf piñon pine, Sandia coral bells, and desert moss. Attracts bees and butterflies. Deer resistant.

NATIVE RANGE AND ORIGIN
This plant occurred in the garden of horticultural expert Ray Daugherty. It is a hybrid between *Heterotheca jonesii*, one of Utah's lesser-known species, and *H. villosa*, a common roadside plant throughout the central and western United States and southern Canada.

Heuchera pulchella

Sandia coral bells • Saxifragaceae (saxifrage family)

SIZE ▸ 3 in. tall (8–10 in. in bloom), 3–8 in. wide

FLOWERS ▸ pink, late spring through early summer

BEST FEATURES ▸ delicate sprays of pink flowers and low-growing evergreen foliage

This choice miniature coral bell is very tough, forming a tidy evergreen mat of leaves. It's often considered to be the most handsome of all coral bells. Thriving in dry shade and on rocky slopes, it offers its fragrant pink flowers when many rock garden plants are starting to fade.

CULTURE

Full sun, partial shade, or shade. Well-drained loam or sandy soil. Moderate watering to dry; xeric in shade. Very low maintenance. Deadhead after flowering to tidy appearance. Rejuvenate older plants through division. Propagate by seed, cuttings, or divisions. USDA hardiness zones 4–7.

LANDSCAPE USE

This is a great plant for troughs, rock gardens, and fairy gardens. It thrives in dry shade and can be a wonderful choice for difficult areas. Spreading slowly, it looks lovely cascading down a rocky slope or over the edge of a trough or permanent container. Combine it with dwarf piñon pine, Blue Jazz single-leaf piñon pine, and oxlip primrose in shadier spots. Attracts bees and hummingbirds. Deer resistant.

NATIVE RANGE AND ORIGIN

Heuchera pulchella is native to mountains of central New Mexico. The plants currently in cultivation can be traced back to a 1992 collection by Panayoti Kelaidis and Gwen Moore.

Iris hookeri

Dwarf beach-head iris • Syn. *Iris setosa* subsp. *canadensis* • Iridaceae (iris family)

SIZE ▶ 8–12 in. tall and wide

FLOWERS ▶ blue, spring

BEST FEATURES ▶ large blue flowers; clean erect clumping foliage

Tidy growth, clean green foliage, porcelain blue flowers, and an upright growth habit make this iris the perfect companion for lower groundcovers. It seems to get better with age and seldom outgrows its allotted space.

CULTURE

Full sun to partial shade. Loam or sandy soil. Moderate watering to dry. Cut back spent flowers and give plants some extra water in the spring before flowering. It will excel in sandy soil if given supplemental watering. Propagate by seeds, which germinate well after a 60-day cold stratification period, or by dividing plants after flowering. USDA hardiness zones 3–8.

LANDSCAPE USE

Clean, nearly grassy, upright foliage provides a textural accent for rock gardens and permanent containers. Vibrant blue flowers have a pleasing sculptural look that will liven up any small border perennial planting, rock garden, or permanent container. It is an excellent accent up against rocks and small boulders. Pair its season-long grasslike foliage with carpeting plants such as desert moss and Sandia coral bells, or with other spring-flowering plants such as miniature columbines. Attracts bees. Deer resistant.

NATIVE RANGE AND ORIGIN

Eastern North American coastal areas.

Pinus edulis dwarf selections

Dwarf piñon pine • Pinaceae (pine family)

SIZE ▸ 24–30 in. tall and wide

FLOWERS ▸ none

BEST FEATURES ▸ evergreen foliage; compact form; edible nuts

Dwarf piñon pines are selections from our native piñons that grow very slowly, about 1–3 in. per year. Named 'Farmy', 'Trinidad', 'Little Jake', 'Peñasco', and 'Tiny Rations', they all possess tight, bright green needles and a compact, rounded growth habit. Cones will form after about ten years of growth. An interesting isolated stand of trees north of Fort Collins at Owl Canyon is thought to have arisen from an accidental dropping of nuts from an indigenous trading party, hence the establishment of this stand of trees 100 miles north of its natural range.

CULTURE
Full sun. Loam or sandy soil. Dry to xeric. Avoid overwatering once the plant is established. Propagate clones by grafting them onto seedling rootstocks. USDA hardiness zones 4–7.

LANDSCAPE USE
The slow growth and compact evergreen forms allow dwarf piñon pines to fit into tight spaces; perfect for rock gardens and permanent containers. These native piñons can easily be used in place of the common nonnative mugo pine and its selections, as they will seldom outgrow their planting site as mugos commonly do. They are extremely drought tolerant, adapt well to harsh conditions, and will grow in higher altitude mountain communities throughout the West. Dwarf piñon pines combine well with most of the Plant Select Petites, as well as with other dryland rock garden and dwarf plants. Deer resistant.

NATIVE RANGE AND ORIGIN
Pinus edulis is native to the foothills of southern Colorado, New Mexico, Arizona, and Utah. The piñon miniatures were collected and brought into cultivation by Jerry Morris, a noted Denver plantsman, from genetically mutated dwarf growths called witches' brooms.

Pinus monophylla 'Blue Jazz'

Blue Jazz single-leaf piñon pine • Pinaceae (pine family)

SIZE ▶ 24–30 in. tall and wide

FLOWERS ▶ none

BEST FEATURES ▶ compact form; blue evergreen foliage; xeric

'Blue Jazz' is the most ornamental of the dwarf piñon pines collected by Jerry Morris and introduced into cultivation. Dwarf globe shape, true blue needle color, and xeric nature make this conifer a great addition to the Plant Select Petites program. Single-leaf piñon pines (*Pinus monophylla* selections) differ from common piñon pines (*P. edulis* selections) in needle color (blue vs. green) and number of needles (usually one vs. two or more per bundle).

CULTURE

Full sun. Loam or sandy soil. Dry to xeric. Very little maintenance required. Avoid overwatering or planting it in a shady location. Propagate by grafting onto seedling rootstocks. USDA hardiness zones 4–7.

LANDSCAPE USE

This slow-growing little blue conifer is the perfect addition to any garden that needs a permanent small evergreen statement for the herbaceous plants to revolve around and play off of. It is an excellent choice for rock gardens, raised beds, large containers, and fairy gardens. It pairs well with Turquoise Tails blue sedum, mock bearberry manzanita, and Scott's sugarbowls. Deer resistant.

NATIVE RANGE AND ORIGIN

The species is native to foothills of Nevada, Utah, Arizona, California, and New Mexico, and this particular form of it was collected by Denver plantsman Jerry Morris from genetically mutated dwarf growths called witches' broom.

Primula elatior

Oxlip primrose • Primulaceae (primrose family)

SIZE ▶ 8–12 in. tall, 12–15 in. wide

FLOWERS ▶ yellow, spring

BEST FEATURES ▶ soft yellow-clustered flowers above rosettes of fresh green foliage; one of the first and most dependable perennials to bloom in light shade; longer blooming than many spring-blooming perennials; much longer-lived than many primroses

Oxlip primrose was chosen as one of three plants to launch the Plant Select Petites program in 2013 for its charm, ease of culture, and shade tolerance. Much more adaptable than most *Primula* species, it tolerates more heat and drought than most, and is less vulnerable to spider mite and slug attacks. The common name has nothing to do with the lip of an ox; *slip* (or *slyppe*) means "dung" in Old Saxon. In its wild haunts in England it showed a propensity for growing noticeably well around old dung piles in meadows. Cowslip is the common name for a primrose with similar haunts and predilections.

Oxlip primrose has been grown in the Rock Alpine Garden at Denver Botanic Gardens since the early 1980s.

CULTURE

Light shade, but tolerates full sun if given more water. Clay, loam, or sandy soil. Moderate watering in full sun; can tolerate dry shade. Cut back finished flower stalks in late spring to refresh the appearance. Remove any tattered leaves in late summer and last season's dead ones in early spring if needed. Propagate by stratified seed or by division of older, bulky, mature rosettes. USDA hardiness zones 4–8.

LANDSCAPE USE

Use oxlip primrose along pathways, patios, in rock gardens, or under smaller trees for spring color. For a fresh spring show in the shade, combine it with spring-blooming soft-colored perennials such as Sandia coral bells or lungwort (*Pulmonaria* spp.). It's also nice with pale-colored dwarf daffodil selections and soft shades of bulbous *Corydalis solida*. Attracts bees. Deer resistant.

NATIVE RANGE AND ORIGIN

Europe and eastern Asia.

Pterocephalus depressus

Moroccan pincushion flower • Dipsacaceae (teasel family)

SIZE ▶ 3 in. tall, 12 in. wide

FLOWERS ▶ pink, late spring through summer

BEST FEATURES ▶ dusty rose-pink flowers; mats of gray-green evergreen foliage; xeric

This native of the Atlas Mountains possesses many ornamental characteristics—low matlike evergreen grayish leaves, short-stemmed pincushion-like pink flowers, and attractive silvery seed heads. It is truly a four-season stunner.

CULTURE
Full sun to very partial shade. Well-drained sandy or amended clay soil. Moderate watering to xeric. Needs little maintenance. Remove occasional dead stems in spring after new growth has emerged. Keep faster-growing plants from overgrowing this treasure. Propagate by division of plants after flowering or by sowing fresh seed. USDA hardiness zones 4–8.

LANDSCAPE USE
This slow-growing groundcover performs best when planted in a rock garden, large container, raised bed, or xeriscape. It loves well-drained soil and sunny hot spots in the garden. It is especially attractive flowing between rocks or boulders where it will fill empty spaces with its charming form, texture, and color. Winter interest is provided by the uniquely textured evergreen foliage. Good companion plants include Blue Jazz single-leaf piñon pine, PURPLE MOUNTAIN sun daisy, and Smoky Hills skullcap. Attracts bees. Deer resistant.

NATIVE RANGE AND ORIGIN
Atlas Mountains of Morocco.

GROUNDCOVERS

Callirhoe involucrata

Winecups • Malvaceae (mallow family)

SIZE ▸ 8–12 in. tall, 48–60 in. wide

FLOWERS ▸ magenta to rose-pink, late spring until hard frost

BEST FEATURES ▸ vibrant flower color; long-blooming; easy to grow; exceptionally drought tolerant; attractive lobed to deeply dissected foliage

After early propagation challenges were met to the satisfaction of member growers, Plant Select first promoted winecups in 1999. This showy native was chosen for its outstanding ornamental characteristics, including its continuous succession of magenta cup-shaped flowers and its dark green palmate leaves. Winecups has proven to be an incredibly durable landscape plant throughout the West.

CULTURE

Full sun to partial shade. Well-drained clay, loam, or sandy soil; tolerates wide pH range. Moderate watering to xeric. Plant with the crown at or slightly above ground level to prevent potential rot. Cut stems back after they turn brown. Water twice per month or as needed to encourage continuous bloom and good growth. A large taproot develops with age; transplanting is generally successful when attempted very early in the growing season or during dormancy. Propagate by seeds, which should be physically scarified or softened with a hot water treatment prior to sowing. Cover lightly with soil. Germination should occur in 3–7 days. Alternatively, direct sow in the fall; flowers occur the second year of growth. USDA hardiness zones 3–9.

LANDSCAPE USE

Winecups is a tough native perennial that thrives in hot sunny spots and is useful as a groundcover or accent in a perennial border, in a native landscape, or scrambling among rocks. It self-sows freely. The bright chalice-shaped flowers look particularly beautiful intermingled with grasses, orange butterfly weed (*Asclepias tuberosa*), and rudbeckia. Attracts bees, butterflies, and moths; an excellent nectar source.

NATIVE RANGE AND ORIGIN

Wyoming, Colorado, North Dakota, and Minnesota south to northern Mexico; concentrated in the central United States as well as Oregon, Michigan, Pennsylvania, and Virginia.

Cynodon 'PWIN04S'

DOG TUFF grass • Poaceae (grass family)

SIZE ▸ 2½–4 in. tall, 2+ ft. wide

FLOWERS ▸ inconspicuous, summer

BEST FEATURES ▸ extremely drought tolerant; soft to touch; bright green in summer; tolerates moderate traffic; resistant to dog urine spotting

This hybrid selection of South African dogtooth grass has been used in the Denver area for many years in private gardens. Its low-care features, low water needs, velvety soft texture, and use in areas where dogs frequent all make it a good option for many situations.

CULTURE

Full sun. Clay, loam or sandy soil. Moderate watering to xeric. Low maintenance. Requires very little water once established and requires little mowing. Left unmowed, DOG TUFF grows in gentle mounds which look somewhat like woodland moss. Because it spreads by runners be sure to site carefully, especially where it won't spread into other turf grasses. Once established, most weeds are often choked out. Propagate by division or stem cuttings. USDA hardiness zones 5–10.

LANDSCAPE USE

DOG TUFF grass is an extremely water-thrifty, warm-season turf grass for hot, sunny spots. An excellent groundcover for slopes and areas with moderate traffic because it recovers quickly after use. As a warm-season grass it takes on a strawlike, tan hue from first to last frost but holds substance throughout winter. Attracts honeybees.

NATIVE RANGE AND ORIGIN

Cynodon species are native to South Africa. DOG TUFF, a sterile hybrid, became popular when Kelly Grummons, a Denver horticulturist, coined the name after observing how well it held up to dog use at his own home.

Delosperma 'Alan's Apricot'

Alan's Apricot ice plant • Aizoaceae (mesembryanthemum family)

SIZE ▶ 1–2 in. tall, 14–18 in. wide

FLOWERS ▶ apricot fading to pink from late spring through early fall

BEST FEATURES ▶ long season of bloom; low-growing succulent

This superior form of hardy ice plant has larger (2-inch) showy blooms covering the foliage nearly all summer long. Flower color changes seasonally from a true orangey-apricot to soft orangey-pink and then back again. One of most cold-hardy of the delospermas.

CULTURE
Full sun, partial shade. Well-drained loam, or sandy soil; does best with excellent drainage. Moderate watering to dry. Needs little care. Site to avoid prolonged periods of snow cover. Propagate by cuttings. USDA hardiness zones 4–9.

LANDSCAPE USE
Hardy ice plants make ideal small-scale groundcovers due to their neat habit and ability to suppress less-vigorous weeds. They also make a wonderful edging to perennial borders, as well as specimens perched in a rock garden or wall. Provide occasional water in very hot and dry conditions. Alan's Apricot combines well with other ice plants, baby blue rabbitbrush, and as a living mulch between sun-loving shrubs and perennials such as agastaches, penstemons, and salvias. Attracts bees and hummingbirds. Deer resistant.

NATIVE RANGE AND ORIGIN
Delospermas are native to South Africa, but Alan's Apricot was discovered as a chance seedling by Alan Tower, Tower Nursery, Spokane, Washington.

Delosperma dyeri 'Psdold'

RED MOUNTAIN ice plant • Aizoaceae (mesembryanthemum family)

SIZE ▸ 1–2 in. tall, 10–14 in. wide

FLOWERS ▸ red with a creamy white center, in early summer

BEST FEATURES ▸ burnished red petals fade to coppery red; dense succulent groundcover

RED MOUNTAIN was the first of this color to be introduced to the U.S. market. Somewhat more compact than the other delospermas, it will be covered with a succession of flowers in early summer. The subtlety of the bright color of the new blooms combined with the older, fading blossoms adds beautiful depth and complexity.

CULTURE
Full sun, partial shade. Well-drained loam or sandy soil. Provide excellent drainage. Moderate watering to dry. Very low care groundcover. Benefits from extra water in late summer during prolonged hot, dry periods. Propagate by cuttings. USDA hardiness zones 5–8.

LANDSCAPE USE
Plant this compact grower in drifts or small groupings along walkways or in the front of perennial borders. Combine it with other hardy other ice plants. It combines exceptionally well with LITTLE TRUDY catmint, dwarf beach-head iris, COLORADO GOLD gazania, and KANNAH CREEK buckwheat. Attracts bees and hummingbirds. Deer resistant.

NATIVE RANGE AND ORIGIN
Selected from a group of seedlings grown from a wild collection made in the Eastern Cape of South Africa for its brilliant red flowers.

Delosperma floribundum

STARBURST ice plant • Aizoaceae (mesembryanthemum family)

SIZE ▶ 4 in. tall, 8–12 in. wide

FLOWERS ▶ purplish pink with a white center, in early summer through summer

BEST FEATURES ▶ bright flowers with a strong-contrasting white center; long-blooming

STARBURST is a slightly mounding and less spreading form of hardy ice plant, grown for its long season of color, adaptability to hot, dry conditions, and cheerfully bright blossoms.

CULTURE

Full sun, partial shade. Well-drained loam or sandy soil; requires excellent drainage, especially in winter. Moderate watering to dry; extra water in late summer helps to prolong bloom period. Easy care succulent groundcover. Propagate by cuttings or seed. USDA hardiness zones 5–9.

LANDSCAPE USE

As a more compact plant, STARBURST should be planted along walkways, as edging to perennial borders, in masses, and in rock gardens or containers. The large white eye adds distinctiveness to mass plantings of mixed ice plants. Combine with PIKE'S PEAK PURPLE, RED ROCKS, WINDWALKER Garnet, or Carolyn's Hope penstemons. Attracts bees and hummingbirds. Deer resistant.

NATIVE RANGE AND ORIGIN

Introduced into cultivation by Panayoti Kelaidis, Denver Botanic Gardens, from seed collected in Free State province of South Africa in 1996.

Delosperma 'John Proffitt'

TABLE MOUNTAIN ice plant • Aizoaceae (mesembryanthemum family)

SIZE ▸ 1–2 in. tall, 16–20 in. wide

FLOWERS ▸ fuchsia-colored with a small white center, in early summer through summer

BEST FEATURES ▸ lustrous flowers; adaptability to a wider range of sites; long-blooming; purple-tinged foliage in winter

One of the easiest to grow, this vigorous form of hardy ice plant offers a long season of bright color and bluish green, ground-hugging succulent foliage that takes on a purplish hue in winter—truly a four-season garden plant.

CULTURE

Full sun, partial shade. Well-drained loam or sandy soil. Moderate watering to dry; extra water in late summer helps prolong bloom period. Needs little care. Propagate by cuttings. USDA hardiness zones 4–9.

LANDSCAPE USE

Easy to grow and adaptable, use as a shallow-rooted living groundcover in perennial and shrub borders, along pathways, tumbling down rock walls, and in larger rock gardens and containers. Attracts bees and hummingbirds. Deer resistant.

NATIVE RANGE AND ORIGIN

Parent seed of this plant was collected by Panayoti Kelaidis, Denver Botanic Gardens, from a vigorous ground-covering form found in the foothills of the Drakensberg mountains of South Africa in 1996.

Delosperma 'Kelaidis'

MESA VERDE ice plant ● Aizoaceae (mesembryanthemum family)

SIZE ▶ 1–2 in. tall, 10–14 in. wide

FLOWERS ▶ pink with pale yellow center, early summer

BEST FEATURES ▶ iridescent salmon-pink-flowers; compact and floriferous

A compact yet vigorous grower, MESA VERDE offers stunning carpets of pink flowers in early summer. The bright green, congested succulent foliage stays attractive until turning bronze-red fall through winter.

CULTURE

Full sun, partial shade. Well-drained loam or sandy soil. Delospermas need excellent drainage, especially in winter and in areas with snow cover. Moderate watering to dry. Little care is needed other than to remove dead stems in spring before new growth emerges. Propagate by cuttings. Commercial propagation of this patented plant is restricted to licensed growers. USDA hardiness zones 4–8.

LANDSCAPE USE

Plant MESA VERDE in the foreground of a perennial border, in trough gardens, cascading over walls or boulders, along walkways, and in rock gardens. Combine with other early summer bloomers such as the Mexicali penstemons and other ice plants. Especially attractive planted with blue-flowering Narbonne blue flax, LITTLE TRUDY catmint, and dwarf beach-head iris. Attracts bees and hummingbirds. Deer resistant.

NATIVE RANGE AND ORIGIN

A spontaneous hybrid between a dwarf high-altitude form of *Delosperma cooperi* and *D. nubigenum* or *D. basuticum*, all species native to South Africa. It appeared in trial plots at Denver Botanic Gardens in 1997 and was named for Panayoti Kelaidis at Denver Botanic Gardens.

Delosperma 'P001S'

FIRE SPINNER ice plant • Aizoaceae (mesembryanthemum family)

SIZE ▶ 1–2 in. tall, 14–18 in. wide

FLOWERS ▶ multitoned in late spring; often a secondary smaller rebloom later in summer

BEST FEATURES ▶ spectacular spring bloom; apple-green succulent foliage all summer

FIRE SPINNER was the first of the cold-hardy, multihued flowering delospermas to be introduced to the U.S. market. A vigorous spreader, the plants flower heavily in late spring then periodically through the summer. Late-season blossoms are usually smaller and more orange-hued.

CULTURE
Full sun, partial shade. Well-drained loam or sandy soil; does best with excellent drainage. Moderate watering to dry. Site to avoid prolonged periods of snow cover. Little care required other than removing dead stems in early spring. Propagate by cuttings. USDA hardiness zones 5–9.

LANDSCAPE USE
Plant where the spectacular blossoms can be appreciated up close— along a walkway, cascading down rock walls, or edging a perennial or shrub border. Use as a groundcover around ornamental grasses; it's also an excellent addition to a larger rock garden as well. Beautiful when planted to contrast with the silvers of Sea Foam sage or the dark foliage of purple smokebush. Attracts bees and hummingbirds. Deer resistant.

NATIVE RANGE AND ORIGIN
The genus traces back to the Eastern Cape of South Africa, but FIRE SPINNER is a selection of unknown parentage brought to Plant Select through Panayoti Kelaidis.

Delosperma 'Psfave'

Lavender Ice ice plant ● Aizoaceae (mesembryanthemum family)

SIZE ▶ 1–2 in. tall, 14–18 in. wide

FLOWERS ▶ lavender with a darker eye in early summer

BEST FEATURES ▶ large blooms with iridescent color; foliage turns purplish in winter

Seeing a patch of Lavender Ice in full bloom is likely to take your breath away. Aptly named, the shimmering pastel-colored flowers shimmer in full sunlight as if covered with ice crystals. One of the easiest of the hardy ice plants to grow and one of the more cold-hardy.

CULTURE
Full sun, partial shade. Well-drained loam or sandy soil; does best with excellent drainage. Moderate watering to dry. Very low care. Does not do well in areas with prolonged snow cover. Propagate by cuttings. USDA hardiness zones 4–9.

LANDSCAPE USE
This vigorous grower should be planted in sunny, dry areas that offer room to grown. Excellent cascading down rock walls or in combination with masses of other ice plants. The lavender blossoms blend beautifully with purple-flowering plants such as PIKE'S PEAK PURPLE and SHADOW MOUNTAIN penstemons, or contrast nicely with the bright yellows of KANNAH CREEK buckwheat or COLORADO GOLD gazania. Attracts bees and hummingbirds. Deer resistant.

NATIVE RANGE AND ORIGIN
Delosperma species are native to South Africa; Lavender Ice was discovered by owners Diana Capen and Merrilee Barnett at Perennial Favorites Nursery in Rye, Colorado, as a sport of TABLE MOUNTAIN ice plant.

Delosperma 'PWWG02S'

RED MOUNTAIN Flame ice plant • Aizoaceae (mesembryanthemum family)

SIZE ▸ 1–2 in. tall, 18–24 in. wide

FLOWERS ▸ red with a purplish center, in early summer

BEST FEATURES ▸ large red flowers with long, narrow petals and a purplish center; vigorous groundcover

This new hybrid selection is a tough, vigorous cold-hardy form with large (2-inch) blazing-orange-red flowers in late spring and early summer. It was selected for superior flower size, unusual flower color, and attractive habit and foliage. The iridescent flowers glow in hot, sunny spots.

CULTURE

Full sun to partial shade. Well-drained loam or sandy soil; excellent drainage is required, especially in winter. Moderate watering to dry. Very low care groundcover. Provide extra water in late summer during prolonged hot, dry periods. Propagate by cuttings. USDA hardiness zones 4–9.

LANDSCAPE USE

One of the more vigorous of the delospermas, plant RED MOUNTAIN Flame where it has room to grow, cascading over rock walls or boulders, or as a groundcover in hot, dry spots. Spectacular when combined with perennials such as red feathers. PIKE'S PEAK PURPLE penstemon, LITTLE TRUDY catmint or COLORADO GOLD gazania. Attracts bees and hummingbirds. Deer resistant.

NATIVE RANGE AND ORIGIN

RED MOUNTAIN Flame was discovered by David Salman, Waterwise Gardening. Santa Fe, New Mexico, in an evaluation row of seedlings.

Eriogonum umbellatum var. *aureum* 'Psdowns'

KANNAH CREEK buckwheat • Polygonaceae (buckwheat family)

SIZE ▶ 12–15 in. tall, 12–24 in. wide

FLOWERS ▶ yellow, summer

BEST FEATURES ▶ bright yellow flowers; persistent deep red foliage in fall; xeric

Flowers are larger and more abundant than the typical species. It has proved itself in cultivation for nearly three decades in the Denver area. The lavish floral display begins in late spring with umbels of bright yellow flowers and extends to midsummer as the persistent petals age to orange and nearly red. KANNAH CREEK buckwheat forms a low mat of deep green leaves that turn a glowing, vivid purple-red in the winter months. It thrives in typical garden culture but also grows well when water is withheld altogether.

CULTURE

Full sun to partial shade. Well-drained clay, loam, or sandy soil. Moderate watering to xeric. Requires very little maintenance when sited properly. May be slow to establish. Does not flourish in areas that are frequently irrigated, poorly drained, or highly amended with organic materials. Propagate by seeds, which germinate well after a 14- to 30-day cold stratification; do not cover as seeds need light to germinate. USDA hardiness zones 3–8.

LANDSCAPE USE

KANNAH CREEK buckwheat makes a great border perennial or groundcover. Plant it individually for accent, or in masses or drifts, among rocks, in the rock garden or xeriscape. Good garden combinations include Mojave sage, LITTLE TRUDY catmint, SILVERTON bluemat penstemon, or Blonde Ambition blue grama grass. Attracts bees, butterflies, moths, and other beneficial insects; an excellent nectar source. Deer resistant.

NATIVE RANGE AND ORIGIN

The species is native to the Western Slope of Colorado near Grand Mesa and is widespread at middle altitudes. This selection was discovered in the 1980s along Kannah Creek near Grand Junction, Colorado, by Dermod Downs.

Marrubium rotundifolium

Silverheels horehound • Lamiaceae (mint family)

SIZE ▸ 4 in. tall, 18–30 in. wide

FLOWERS ▸ white, summer

BEST FEATURES ▸ neat mat-forming plant; clustered whorls of small flowers in summer that attract butterflies; xeric; pest-free

The neat habit and furry foliage characteristic of all marrubiums are easily recognized and appealing, and *Marrubium rotundifolium* is no exception. The small, rounded, medium green leaves are edged in silvery white and have a woolly white underside.

CULTURE

Full sun. Clay, loam, or sandy soil. Moderate watering to xeric. Promptly remove spent flower stems to keep the foliage full and robust. Cut plants back hard in late winter, either to the base if severely dried out and damaged, or by half if the stems are still supple. Propagate by seed or cuttings. USDA hardiness zones 4–9.

LANDSCAPE USE

The soft, semievergreen foliage brings much-needed contrast of texture and fresh green color to other xeric plants. Plant it to soften path edges, cascade down slopes, or drape around rocks. Silverheels horehound is especially nice combined with flashy bloomers such as penstemon, ice plant, salvia, ORANGE CARPET hummingbird trumpet, SUNSET foxglove, and hummingbird trumpet mint. Attracts butterflies and bees. Deer resistant.

NATIVE RANGE AND ORIGIN

Silverheels horehound, a species from Turkey, was trialed by Panayoti Kelaidis in Denver Botanic Gardens' Rock Alpine Garden along with many other Old World mint family plants throughout the 1980s and 1990s. It proved to be one of the hardiest and most attractive, and made its way into the hands of various Denver nurseries and gardeners and to Plant Select.

Paxistima canbyi

Mountain lover • Celastraceae (bittersweet family)

SIZE ▸ 8–12 in. tall, 15–20 in. wide

FLOWERS ▸ inconspicuous, green, spring

BEST FEATURES ▸ tolerates alkaline soil; performs well in dry shade; very useful as an evergreen groundcover beneath large shrubs or trees

This mat-forming, evergreen shrublet is quite rare in its native habitat, though it seems to flourish in cultivation, especially in that most challenging of garden environments—dry shade. Distantly related to euonymous, this unassuming, twiggy groundcover offers year-round interest. The species name commemorates William Marriott Canby, an American philanthropist and botanist in the mid- to late 1800s.

CULTURE

Partial shade to shade. Loam. Moderate watering. Intolerant of foot traffic when grown as a groundcover. Slow growing, so planting closer together result in a faster fill. Needs little care once established. Prune out any dead branches in late spring when new growth is emerging. Propagate by layering stems. Success rate for rooting softwood or hardwood cuttings is low. USDA hardiness zones 4–9.

LANDSCAPE USE

Mountain lover is ideal as a very low hedge, in the foreground of the shade border, in informal plantings or woodland designs. Used primarily as an evergreen groundcover for dry shade, it combines with small-scale shrubs such as MINI MAN dwarf Manchurian viburnum and waxflower, as well as with Korean feather reed grass. Attracts bees. Deer resistant.

NATIVE RANGE AND ORIGIN

Appalachian Mountains of Virginia, West Virginia, Kentucky, into southern Ohio, Pennsylvania, Tennessee, and North Carolina; among calcareous rocks on slopes.

Sedum sediforme

Turquoise Tails blue sedum • Syn. *Petrosedum sediforme* • Crassulaceae (stonecrop family)

SIZE ▶ 6–10 in. tall, 12–18 in. wide

FLOWERS ▶ creamy yellow, early summer

BEST FEATURES ▶ silvery blue evergreen fleshy foliage whorled along semiprostrate stems; stays plump and colorful through winter; flat-topped clusters of starry flowers rise above foliage in mid- to late summer; very xeric; easy care

Turquoise Tails blue sedum is similar but larger in overall size to blue spruce sedum (*Sedum reflexum*) with a brighter blue color year-round, less shriveling in winter, and more drought-, clay- and heat-tolerance. It's especially useful in colder parts of its hardiness range where low-growing winter interest is rare.

CULTURE

Full sun to light shade. Well-drained clay, loam, or sandy soil. Dry to xeric. Cut back finished flower stalks in late summer to refresh plant appearance for autumn. Avoid planting where many falling leaves settle, as it doesn't like winter cover and can't be raked or strongly blown without damage. Propagate by cuttings during active growth. Any broken foliage stems can be stuck directly in the ground where desired to start new plants. USDA hardiness zones 5a–10.

LANDSCAPE USE

Turquoise Tails blue sedum forms a rotund mound of fresh, cool color in the dry garden where its plump texture contrasts with the twigginess of many xeric plants and the harshness of cacti and fiber plants. For best habit, don't crowd it with other plants too close by. Superb as a hardy permanent outdoor container plant, it's also nice on slopes and among rocks. It's useful for softening hard architectural edges, and makes a good roof garden plant. Although it can serve as a slow-spreading groundcover or edge plant, it doesn't tolerate foot traffic or being brushed or bumped. Combine this sedum with other dryland plants that will accent the dusty-blue foliage, such as Blue Jazz single-leaf and other dwarf piñon pines, AUTUMN SAPPHIRE sage, Standing Ovation little bluestem, and KANNAH CREEK buckwheat. Attracts bees. Deer resistant.

NATIVE RANGE AND ORIGIN

Coastal Mediterranean. This form of the plant was pioneered in the Rocky Mountain region by plantspeople Lauren and Scott Ogden and nurseryman Kelly Grummons. Scott received cuttings taken from the steps of the Parthenon in Greece by Texas plantsman Logan Calhoon in the middle 1980s and grew it successfully for many years in his home garden in central Texas. He brought it to Lauren's Fort Collins, Colorado, garden in 2003 where it proved entirely hardy and still thrives.

Tanacetum densum subsp. amani

Partridge feather • Asteraceae (aster family)

SIZE ▶ 4–6 in. tall, 18–24 in. wide

FLOWERS ▶ yellow rayless, summer

BEST FEATURES ▶ soft low mounds of feathery silver foliage that spread slowly over time; golden button flowers in summer; extremely xeric; tolerates dry, bright shade

Silver plants are always beloved, and this one out-silvers most with its irresistible featherlike, soft, almost white foliage. Partridge feather was popularized by its public planting in the Rock Alpine Garden at Denver Botanic Gardens by Panayoti Kelaidis, and as a major theme in the original design of the WaterSmart Garden in the middle 1990s by Lauren Springer Ogden.

CULTURE

Full sun to partial shade. Loam or sandy soil. Dry to xeric. Cut off spent flowers; in spots where thinning or dieback is noted; cut back to almost ground level for dense resprouting. Avoid overhead watering or foliage and stems may rot. It does not do well in rich, clayey soils. Propagate by cuttings in mid- to late summer; do not mist. USDA hardiness zones 4–9.

LANDSCAPE USE

Partridge feather makes a terrific edge plant and unifying theme when threaded throughout a dryland garden. It spreads slowly so it will not overwhelm other low-growing plants. Its soft, feathery silver leaves combine well with VALLEY LAVENDER plains verbena, KANNAH CREEK buckwheat, Gold on Blue prairie zinnia, ORANGE CARPET hummingbird trumpet, chocolate flower, Scott's sugarbowls, SILVER BLADE evening primrose, and penstemons. Deer resistant.

NATIVE RANGE AND ORIGIN

Southeastern Turkey.

Verbena bipinnatifida

VALLEY LAVENDER plains verbena • *Syn. Glandularia bipinnatifida* • Verbenaceae (verbena family)

SIZE ▶ 3–6 in. tall, 12–18 in. wide

FLOWERS ▶ purple, spring through fall

BEST FEATURES ▶ cold hardy; long bloom period; vibrant lavender-purple blooms

Introduced by Plant Select in 2005, VALLEY LAVENDER is highly cold and drought tolerant. Even when it's not flowering heavily, the highly dissected, gray-green foliage is very attractive. With only occasional watering, it can bloom all summer and may even bloom into early winter in mild years.

CULTURE

Full sun. Well-drained clay, loam, or sandy soil. Moderate watering to xeric. Prefers native soil. May not be as cold-hardy in soil with high clay content. Intolerant of heavy shade or excessive watering. Propagate by tip cuttings which easily root. USDA hardiness zones 5–8.

LANDSCAPE USE

VALLEY LAVENDER plains verbena can be used in a rock garden, xeriscape, or meadow, and looks especially nice cascading over a wall or in the front of a dry border. This groundcover looks as good in a formal garden as it does in a wild setting. The luminous lavender flowers combine especially well with bright yellow flowers of KANNAH CREEK buckwheat or Gold on Blue prairie zinnia. It also pairs well with manzanitas and dwarf piñon pine. Attracts butterflies and hummingbirds; a good source of nectar.

NATIVE RANGE AND ORIGIN

The species is native to Great Plains of North America south into Central America, and the strain was developed by Little Valley Wholesale Nursery in Brighton, Colorado.

Veronica liwanensis

Turkish veronica • Scrophulariaceae (figwort family)

SIZE ▶ 1–2 in. tall, 15–32 in. wide

FLOWERS ▶ blue, spring

BEST FEATURES ▶ brilliant blue blossoms for an extended period; tolerates alkaline soil; nearly evergreen foliage

Small, glossy, rounded leaves form a dense mat, covered by a stunning display of small, four-petaled cobalt blue flowers from midspring through early summer. A perfect complement to spring bulbs, it continues to bloom after they're finished. It fills in quickly and vigorously, spreading across the garden by stems which root themselves in the soil. Evergreen leaves turn purplish in winter.

CULTURE

Full sun to partial shade. Clay, loam, or sandy soil. Moderate watering to xeric. Additional irrigation during the heat of summer helps to keep the foliage bright and green. Performs best in well-drained soil. Lightly rake out old leaves in early spring to refresh the plant for spring bloom. Propagate by stem cuttings at any time of year. USDA hardiness zones 3–10.

LANDSCAPE USE

Turkish veronica is a beautiful groundcover among flagstones and patio pavers. It can also be used as a border along a sunny or partly shaded garden, or as filler where spring-blooming bulbs are planted. It is beautiful when combined with SNOW-MASS blue-eyed veronica, TANAGER gazania, KANNAH CREEK buckwheat, or pink soapwort (*Saponaria*). Deer resistant.

NATIVE RANGE AND ORIGIN

Pontiac Mountains in northeastern Turkey, among limestone and igneous rocks, on ledges, in crevices and scree, and in alpine pastures. Introduced by the University of British Columbia expedition to Turkey led by Roy Davidson, James MacPhail, and John Watson in 1977.

Veronica 'Reavis'

CRYSTAL RIVER veronica • Scrophulariaceae (figwort family)

SIZE ▶ 2–3 in. tall, 20–32 in. wide

FLOWERS ▶ blue, late spring through early summer

BEST FEATURES ▶ profusion of bright blue flowers; vigorous spreading habit; xeric

CRYSTAL RIVER is a spontaneous hybrid between *Veronica liwanensis* and *V. pectinata* with the bright green leaves of the former and the vigor of the latter. The evergreen foliage adds winter interest as the leaves have a purplish tinge in the cold months. The medium blue sparkling flowers of CRYSTAL RIVER bloom in late spring to early summer and are timed right between its parents, adding another hue of blue in the spring garden.

CULTURE

Full sun to partial shade. Clay, loam or sandy soil. Moderate watering to xeric. Requires little care. Tolerates low water conditions and alkaline soil. Spreads rapidly but not aggressively. Propagate by stem cuttings or plant divisions. USDA hardiness zones 3–7.

LANDSCAPE USE

CRYSTAL RIVER veronica is an excellent border perennial or groundcover and can be planted either individually for accent or in masses or drifts. It does well in a rock garden or xeriscapes, especially when tucked among rocks or between pavers. Fast growing, it will form a somewhat tight mat fairly quickly. CRYSTAL RIVER veronica is excellent in a rock garden as it cascades down a rock wall or walkway, giving the impression of a blue river. Plant it beneath shrub roses, Engelmann's daisy, or thread-leaf coreopsis (*Coreopsis verticillata*). It combines beautifully with other groundcovers such as KANNAH CREEK buckwheat, and ice plants. Deer resistant.

NATIVE RANGE AND ORIGIN

Found at Denver Botanic Gardens in 1998, this natural hybrid is a cross between two species native to Turkey.

Zinnia grandiflora 'Gold on Blue'

Gold on Blue prairie zinnia • Asteraceae (aster family)

SIZE ▶ 8–10 in. tall, 18 in. wide

FLOWERS ▶ yellow, summer

BEST FEATURES ▶ excellent vigor; blue-green foliage; large golden flowers

A native of the dry Southwest, golden-flowered prairie zinnia dislikes wet conditions and requires hot, arid landscapes, where it will sucker to make colonies, filling in large areas over time. In addition to its vigorous growth habit, this resilient groundcover forms tidy mats of finely textured blue-green foliage covered with golden yellow blooms in late summer.

CULTURE

Full sun. Clay, loam, or sandy soil. Dry to xeric. Needs little care once established. Be sure to plant in late spring or early in summer to allow it to establish a strong crown before winter's cold. Plants spread to fill so give them room to grow. Cut or shear plants back in late fall or spring to clean out the old growth. Propagate by tip cuttings or division of plants. USDA hardiness zones 4–8.

LANDSCAPE USE

Gold on Blue prairie zinnia is an excellent choice for hot, dry locations or for erosion control on dry slopes. Use it for naturalizing and in meadows, or along driveways and in median strips. It also works well in the front of a xeric border, or in a rock garden. Gold on Blue is spectacular with summer bloomers like Mojave sage, LITTLE TRUDY catmint, VALLEY LAVENDER plains verbena, and Standing Ovation little bluestem grass. Attracts bees, birds, moths, and butterflies; good pollen and nectar source. Deer resistant.

NATIVE RANGE AND ORIGIN

Introduced by Plant Select in 2014, this selection of native prairie zinnia (Colorado, Kansas, New Mexico, Arizona, Oklahoma, and Texas) was developed by horticulturist David Salman of Santa Fe, New Mexico, from seedlings of a single plant discovered near Trinidad, Colorado.

PERENNIALS

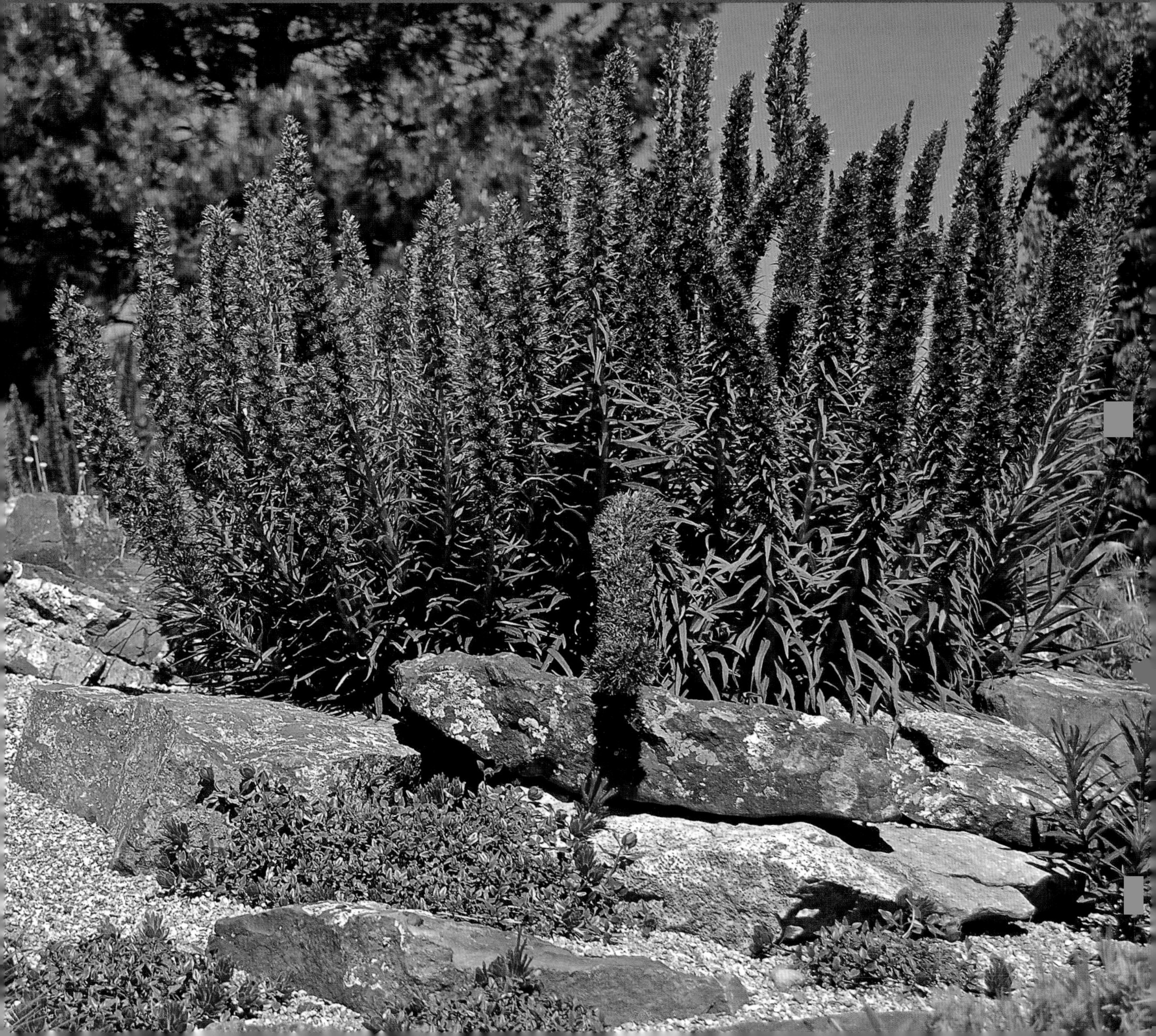

Agastache aurantiaca 'PO12S'

CORONADO hyssop • Lamiaceae (mint family)

SIZE ▶ 15–18 in. tall by 12–15 in. wide

FLOWERS ▶ orange-yellow, summer through fall

BEST FEATURES ▶ brightly colored trumpet flowers in late summer; intensely aromatic foliage; attracts hummingbirds

Perennials that start blooming in late summer and continuing through fall are often overlooked in the passion of spring gardening fever, but CORONADO hyssop in full bloom will give anyone pause to reconsider the necessity of late-summer perennial color.

CULTURE

Full sun to partial shade. Loam or sandy soil; excellent drainage is essential for longevity. Moderate watering to dry. Best planted early in the season. Wait to cut back old stems until new growth is at least 2–3 in. long. Propagate by cuttings. USDA hardiness zones 5–9.

LANDSCAPE USE

When planted in masses, the bounty of flowers is showstopping. Use in foundation plantings, parking strips, or wildflower gardens, as well as traditional perennial borders or even herb gardens. Orange and blue are naturally complementary colors, so combine with plants such as blue avena grass (*Helictotrichon sempervirens*), Standing Ovation little bluestem, AUTUMN SAPPHIRE sage, or Russian sage (*Perovskia atriplicifolia*) for beautiful late-season color. Attracts bees and hummingbirds. Deer resistant.

NATIVE RANGE AND ORIGIN

CORONADO was the first selection made from seed of *Agastache aurantiaca* collected by Sally Walker, a seed collector from Tucson, Arizona. The seedling was chosen for its greater cold-hardiness and billowing clouds of yellow and orange flowers. The species is native throughout northern Mexico, New Mexico and Arizona.

Agastache aurantiaca 'Pstessene'

CORONADO Red hyssop • Lamiaceae (mint family)

SIZE ▸ 15–18 in. tall by 12–15 in. wide

FLOWERS ▸ reddish-orange, summer through fall

BEST FEATURES ▸ brightly colored trumpet flowers in late summer; intensely aromatic foliage; attracts hummingbirds

Seen from a distance, CORONADO Red plants are like clouds of red flowers in the garden, but up close the intricate colors and flower complexity are most appreciated. Providing plants with well-drained soil conditions improves their performance and longevity. Hot, sunny conditions enhance both the color and the abundance of flowers.

CULTURE

Full sun to partial shade. Loam or sandy soil that is well-drained to assure longer-lived plants. Moderate watering to dry. Leave plants standing through winter and wait until late spring when new growth is vigorously growing to cut back last year's stems. Propagate by cuttings. USDA hardiness zones 5–9.

LANDSCAPE USE

CORONADO Red is an excellent perennial for hot, dry, sunny spots such as parking strips and against buildings or walls. Use for late-summer color in perennial or mixed borders, native and habitat gardens. Pairs well with red yucca, AUTUMN SAPPHIRE sage, Standing Ovation little bluestem, and Blonde Ambition blue grama grass for landscape interest from late summer through fall. Attracts bees and hummingbirds. Deer resistant.

NATIVE RANGE AND ORIGIN

This red-flowered selection was discovered at Welby Gardens, Denver, Colorado, among a crop of the original, orange-yellow form of CORONADO hyssop. It carries the same attributes of floriferousness, long flowering period from midsummer into fall, the ability to grow in average garden soil, aromatic foliage, and a superior attraction for bees and hummingbirds in the garden.

Agastache cana 'Sinning'

SONORAN SUNSET hyssop • Lamiaceae (mint family)

SIZE ▶ 15 in. tall, 12–15 in. wide

FLOWERS ▶ bright lavender-rose, summer through fall

BEST FEATURES ▶ brightly colored flowers; intensely aromatic; xeric

The flowers of this cultivar are almost twice the size of the wild species and an even more intense lavender-rose color. It usually begins to bloom in midsummer, and fresh flowers are produced throughout late summer (monsoon season in its native Southwest).

CULTURE

Full sun to partial shade. Loam or sandy soil. Moderate watering to xeric. Hardiness of this plant is maximized if it's planted on a slope, or with the added heat of a nearby rock or wall to reflect heat. Continue to water into late summer or flowering will cease, but taper off irrigation in early autumn since drier winter conditions increase hardiness. Propagate by softwood cuttings, which are relatively easy using a greenhouse or propagation frame. Commercial propagation of this patented plant is restricted to licensed growers. USDA hardiness zones 5–9.

LANDSCAPE USE

A great border perennial, SONORAN SUNSET is a shining star in dry gardens and xeriscapes. It is spectacular when planted with Russian sage (*Perovskia atriplicifolia*) and grasses such as Blonde Ambition blue grama grass, UNDAUNTED ruby muhly, or Standing Ovation little bluestem. It also combines nicely with Tennessee purple coneflower, LAVENDER MIST sun daisy, or SHADOW MOUNTAIN penstemon. Attracts hummingbirds, bees, butterflies, and moths; an excellent nectar source. Deer resistant.

NATIVE RANGE AND ORIGIN

Native to southwestern uplands of Arizona, New Mexico, and Mexico, the wild form of *Agastache cana* was introduced to general horticulture by Plants of the Southwest in the 1970s, when it was purchased by Jim Knopf who publicized the plant and shared it with Denver Botanic Gardens. A superior seedling was selected at Welby Gardens in Denver by Duane Sinning, who's commemorated in the cultivar name.

Agastache rupestris

Sunset hyssop • Lamiaceae (mint family)

SIZE ▶ 20–24 in. tall, 16–20 in. wide

FLOWERS ▶ rusty orange with a pale lavender calyx, summer through fall

BEST FEATURES ▶ distinct appearance with multicolored flower spikes; pleasingly aromatic flowers and foliage; long-blooming; rich nectar source for pollinators; xeric

Since its commercial introduction in 1997, this plant has garnered attention throughout the United States and Europe where its stunning flowers, unique fine-textured foliage, and strong, minty aromatic fragrance have captivated gardeners. This is an indispensable perennial for attracting hummingbirds.

CULTURE

Full sun to partial shade. Well-drained loam or sandy soil. Moderate watering to xeric. Plant in spring in colder climates. Water established plants deeply but infrequently. Cut back in midspring just above the mound of new growth. Leave stems standing over winter to improve cold hardiness. Propagate by seeds, which germinate easily without pretreatment but need bright light and a soil temperature of 70–75°F; cover lightly. Seedlings need excellent air circulation as downy mildew can infect damp foliage. USDA hardiness zones 4b–10.

LANDSCAPE USE

Sunset hyssop is a durable native plant that thrives in hot, dry conditions and needs an infertile, well-drained soil. The plant is very resistant to browsing rabbit and deer. It mixes well into xeriscapes with other water-wise perennials and ornamental grasses and provides several months of invaluable late-summer flowers. It reseeds itself when grown with gravel mulch and will naturalize when given its preferred conditions. Sunset hyssop is stunning when combined with WINDWALKER big bluestem, Standing Ovation little bluestem, regal torchlily, LITTLE TRUDY catmint, SILVER BLADE evening primrose, or Mojave sage. Attracts hummingbirds, hawk moths, and honeybees; an excellent nectar source. Deer resistant.

NATIVE RANGE AND ORIGIN

The wild species is native to limited areas in the mountains of southeastern Arizona, southwestern New Mexico, and Chihuahua, Mexico. Seed for this rare native plant was first offered by Sally Walker of Southwestern Native Seeds and came into limited cultivation in the early 1990s.

Amsonia jonesii

Colorado desert blue star • Apocynaceae (dogbane family)

SIZE ▶ 10–15 in. tall, 12–15 in. wide

FLOWERS ▶ light blue, spring through early summer

BEST FEATURES ▶ steel blue flowers in spring and golden foliage in fall

Colorado desert blue star is a welcome addition to the xeriscape and dryland rock garden because of its great adaptability to the harshest and driest conditions, but with a softer look and feel. Most *Amsonia* species are from wetland or riparian areas, but this western native desert blue star grows in hot, dry areas in habitat with single-leafed ash, desert buckwheat, and several species of cacti. It has wonderful fall color of gold and vivid yellow.

CULTURE

Full sun. Clay, loam, or sandy loam soil. Moderate watering to xeric. Need little maintenance. Cut it back in early winter or in spring before the plant starts to grow. Propagate by seed, which requires at least a 30-day cold stratification. Germination is erratic and can take several months. Also propagate by root cuttings, but allow cuttings to dry for several hours until the plant has finished exuding its milky sap. USDA hardiness zones 4–9.

LANDSCAPE USE

Colorado desert blue star is an easy-care filler plant for a wide range of gardens, including rock gardens, xeriscapes, and dry perennial borders. Good pairings for it are dwarf piñon pine, chocolate flower, and red feathers, and it's stunning combined with orange California poppies (*Eschscholzia californica*). Attracts bees, butterflies, and moths. Deer resistant.

NATIVE RANGE AND ORIGIN

Western Slope of Colorado, around the Four Corners region and into eastern Utah and northern Arizona.

Anchusa capensis

Summer forget-me-not, Cape forget-me-not • Boraginaceae (borage family)

SIZE ▸ 8–15 in. tall, 4–8 in. wide

FLOWERS ▸ cobalt blue, spring through fall

BEST FEATURES ▸ striking flower color; long-blooming; attractive foliage

The piercing cobalt blue spikes of forget-me-not can start to bloom in midspring, lasting throughout the summer into fall. The trim rosettes of dark blue, strap-shaped leaves make attractive patterns even when the plant is not in bloom. It will naturalize with moderate self-sowing.

CULTURE
Full sun to partial shade. Clay, loam, or sandy loam soil. Moderate watering. Plant in spring for blooms in summer and into the fall with some deadheading. Allow some of the stems to go to seed to produce more plants around the parents. Propagate by seeds which germinate well after a 14- to 30-day cold stratification; do not cover as seeds need light to germinate. USDA hardiness zones 5–10.

LANDSCAPE USE
The summer forget-me-not is an adaptable, clump-forming perennial that performs well in a variety of sites and soils. Surprisingly tough, it can bloom within months of sowing the seed, making it worth growing as an annual in colder areas where it usually doesn't survive winter. In many gardens, it can self-sow moderately to make stunning patches of color, and it looks lovely when growing in small drifts. Since it's slightly informal in its habit, it does not look its best in strictly linear plantings. Orange and blue are classic combinations, so plantings with orange California poppies (*Eschscholzia californica*), regal torchlily, and TANAGER gazania are guaranteed winners. Attracts bees, butterflies, and moths; an excellent nectar source. Deer resistant.

NATIVE RANGE AND ORIGIN
Much of southern Africa at various elevations.

Anthemis marschalliana

Filigree daisy • Asteraceae (aster family)

SIZE ▸ 4 in. tall (12 in. in bloom), 12–18 in. wide

FLOWERS ▸ yellow, spring

BEST FEATURES ▸ feathery mat of gray foliage with deep yellow daisies, making for a lovely silver-and-gold combination; needs minimal tending; long-lived in dry conditions

Daisies are ever-popular, as is fine-textured silver foliage, making the filigree daisy a winning combination. Most *Anthemis* species are aromatic and quite xeric, many are annuals or short-lived perennials, and some are potentially invasive, but filigree daisy, being both well-behaved and beautiful, is one of the best of the genus. In dry sunny climates it is as easy to grow as common catmint, but without the seeding issues.

CULTURE

Full sun to partial shade. Well-drained clay or sandy soil. Moderate watering to xeric. Deadhead spent flowers in summer to encourage new foliage growth. Also grows in loam soil if not overfertilized. Propagate by seed, division, or cuttings. USDA hardiness zones 4–10.

LANDSCAPE USE

The low-growing, neat mat of foliage makes for a superb edging plant as well as rock garden specimen. It is excellent in naturalistic xeric gardens as well as in more flowery dry cottage gardens. It's also a candidate for roof gardens. Combine filigree daisy with Turquoise Tails blue sedum, VALLEY LAVENDER plains verbena, Scott's sugarbowls, Narbonne blue flax, LITTLE TRUDY catmint, or PLATINUM sage.

NATIVE RANGE AND ORIGIN

Northeastern Turkey, southern Caucasus region.

Aquilegia chrysantha

DENVER GOLD columbine • Ranunculaceae (buttercup family)

SIZE ▶ 30–36 in. tall, 15–20 in. wide

FLOWERS ▶ yellow, late spring through summer

BEST FEATURES ▶ long season of bloom; adaptable to various soils and conditions; much more stable in flower color and habit than other columbines and less likely to hybridize

Columbines are popular in regional gardens, and Rocky Mountain columbine (*Aquilegia caerulea*), the Colorado state flower, is especially cherished. Golden columbine (*Aquilegia chrysantha*), another regional native, is adaptable to a wide range of light conditions as well as soil types. One form of it, DENVER GOLD columbine, thrives in sunny conditions, but also does well in partly shaded areas. The flowers continue for weeks on end and the plants are longer-lived than most other columbines.

CULTURE

Full sun to partial shade. Clay, loam, or sandy soil. Moderate watering, but grows well in dry shade. Avoid overhead watering to prevent development of powdery mildew, especially during the hotter months. Deadhead faded flowers consistently to encourage continuous flowering into summer. Propagate by seed, which germinates relatively easy; use the freshest seed possible and give a 14-day cold, moist stratification before sowing. USDA hardiness zones 3–8.

LANDSCAPE USE

Use DENVER GOLD columbine in perennial borders or allow it to naturalize in shaded areas. Its yellow flowers pair well with Cape-forget-me-not, Cashmere sage, Corsican violet, and Korean feather reed grass. Attracts butterflies and hawk moths.

NATIVE RANGE AND ORIGIN

DENVER GOLD is a selection of *Aquilegia chrysantha*, which is native to Colorado, Utah, Arizona, New Mexico, Texas, and northwestern Mexico.

Aquilegia 'Swan Violet & White'

REMEMBRANCE columbine • Ranunculaceae (buttercup family)

SIZE ▶ 14–24 in. tall, 15–18 in. wide

FLOWERS ▶ violet-blue with white, late spring through late summer

BEST FEATURES ▶ striking deep violet-blue and pure white flowers; attractive foliage

REMEMBRANCE columbine was named in memory of the victims of the Columbine High School tragedy in 1999 in Littleton, Colorado. It features deep violet-blue sepals and spurs, pure white petals, and prominent golden stamens.

CULTURE
Partial sun. Well-drained loam. Moderate watering. Remove spent flowers consistently to encourage prolonged blooming. Keep soil moist to prolong bloom time. Foliage often declines by midsummer, at which point it should be cut to the ground and allowed to regrow. The plant may self-seed and hybridize with other nearby aquilegias and may be short-lived. Propagate by seed. Most commercially available seeds of this columbine are already pretreated and will germinate readily. It will not come consistently true from seeds produced in the garden. USDA hardiness zones 3–9.

LANDSCAPE USE
Use REMEMBRANCE columbine as a border perennial for shaded or partially shaded areas with morning sun only. Combine it with DENVER GOLD columbine, alpine willowherb, and other partial shade plants, such as bergenias, *Corydalis lutea*, and dark-leaved coral bells. Attracts bees.

NATIVE RANGE AND ORIGIN
This selection comes from the Songbird columbine series produced by Ball Horticultural Company. The female and male parents were developed by Charlie Weddle and Ellen Leue, respectively, with *Aquilegia caerulea* (native to Rocky Mountains) and *A. canadensis* (native from Nova Scotia to Florida, west to Minnesota and Tennessee) being key species in the mix.

Artemisia versicolor 'Sea Foam'

Sea Foam sage • Syn. *Artemisia alba* 'Canescens' • Asteraceae (aster family)

SIZE ▸ 8–12 in. tall, 20–36 in. wide

FLOWERS ▸ inconspicuous, greenish white, summer

BEST FEATURES ▸ fine-textured, filigreed silver foliage; does not spread aggressively; vigorous and appealing all year; long-lived; exceptionally xeric; adaptable; easy care

The beautiful, uniquely lichenlike silver foliage of this artemisia and its noninvasive character make it an indispensable plant for dry western gardens. It has been grown in mild West Coast gardens for some time but cold hardiness was not known until Lauren Springer Ogden successfully grew cuttings in her zone 4b Windsor, Colorado, garden.

CULTURE

Full sun to partial shade. Well-drained clay, loam, or sandy soil. Moderate watering to xeric. Cut back flower stalks when they detract from the foliage appearance. Cut back woody stems by about a third in late winter to promote dense, compact growth. Do not overhead irrigate regularly or foliage may rot. Plant in full sun for best form and color. Propagate by cuttings or by removing and planting rooted prostrate stems; use mist sparingly or not. USDA hardiness zone 4.

LANDSCAPE USE

Use Sea Foam sage as either an anchor or a repeated theme. It can be useful on hillsides, to soften architectural features, or as an edge planting along paths. It combines well with bright flower colors as well as pastels, and goes with practically any plant that thrives with similar culture. Some good combinations are SILVER BLADE evening primrose, winecups, UNDAUNTED ruby muhly, sulfur flower, manzanitas, penstemons, ORANGE CARPET hummingbird trumpet, and Avalanche white sun daisy. Deer resistant.

NATIVE RANGE AND ORIGIN

Artemisia versicolor is native to southern Europe and North Africa, and Sea Foam is a selection of it grown from cuttings Lauren Springer Ogden brought back from England in 1989.

Berlandiera lyrata

Chocolate flower • Asteraceae (aster family)

SIZE ▶ 10–20 in. tall and wide

FLOWERS ▶ bright yellow, summer until hard frost

BEST FEATURES ▶ fragrant, brightly colored flowers; long-blooming

Chocolate flower lives up to its vernacular name. The fragrance in the early morning and late afternoon is of rich dark chocolate. After flowering, the chartreuse seed heads provide further texture to a display. The long flowering period adds color and fragrance through the summer.

CULTURE
Full sun. Well-drained clay or sandy soil. Dry to xeric. With this plant the best maintenance practice is prevention. Avoid overwatering and too much shading to keep plants compact and blooming heavily. Fall cleanup prevents plants from seeding around excessively. Propagate by seeds, which germinate well; do not cover as seeds need light to germinate. USDA hardiness zones 4–9.

LANDSCAPE USE
When growing alone in a garden, chocolate flower can be a mounding perennial, but if it's grown in a mixed garden with grasses and other xeric perennials, it can be sprawling and will intertwine with other plants as support for what could otherwise be floppy growth. It combines especially well with desert beardtongue, Scott's sugarbowls, LITTLE TRUDY catmint, VALLEY LAVENDER plains verbena, Blonde Ambition blue grama grass, and Standing Ovation little bluestem. Attracts butterflies and other beneficial insects. Deer resistant.

NATIVE RANGE AND ORIGIN
Southwestern United States.

Clematis integrifolia 'PSHarlan'

MONGOLIAN BELLS clematis • Ranunculaceae (buttercup family)

SIZE ▶ 10–15 in. tall, 12–15 in. wide

FLOWERS ▶ a mix of blue, lavender, white, and pink, spring through summer

BEST FEATURES ▶ very prolific reblooming perennial when deadheaded or cut back

This collection is more compact than the straight species, making it less floppy and a better fit for the garden. It is a very beautiful and adaptable perennial.

CULTURE

Full sun to partial shade. Loam or sandy soil. Moderate watering to dry. Deadhead or cut back after blooming; may rebloom several times a season. Propagate by seeds, which germinate well after a 30-day cold stratification; do not cover as seeds need light to germinate. USDA hardiness zones 3–9.

LANDSCAPE USE

MONGOLIAN BELLS clematis is most effective when planted in drifts or in clumps of multiples, maximizing the potential for the widest range of color combinations. Plant it where it is easy to get to because it readily reblooms when deadheaded. It combines nicely with many early summer-blooming, water-wise perennials, including filigree daisy, DENVER GOLD columbine, Dalmatian daisy, and Cashmere sage. Deer resistant.

NATIVE RANGE AND ORIGIN

The species is native to central Asia, and the selection was originally collected in Mongolia by the late plant explorer Harlan Hamernik of Bluebird Nursery, where it was grown and distributed but was eventually lost. A large planting at the Denver Botanic Gardens in the PlantAsia Garden included all of the color variations and became the new standard and the seed source that supplied the reintroduction and revival of this clematis.

Crambe maritima

Curly leaf sea kale • Brassicaceae (mustard family)

SIZE ▶ 18–24 in. tall, 30–48 in. wide

FLOWERS ▶ white, late spring through early summer

BEST FEATURES ▶ purplish-blue ruffled foliage in spring; wavy-edged turquoise blue leaves in summer; large panicles of small white flowers; adaptable; long-lived

Sea kale is grown as both an edible and ornamental in England where it also is native. It is a strong-tasting cruciferous vegetable, best blanched as young leaves and stems. After almost two decades in the Colorado nursery trade, curly leaf sea kale's stunning foliage, adaptability, well behaved nature, and longevity finally brought it Plant Select renown.

CULTURE

Full sun. Well-drained clay, loam, or sandy soil. Moderate to dry. Cut back finished flower stalks in summer to refresh the appearance. Remove leaves as they age and new ones emerge. Foliage can be marred in overly damp sites by slugs and occasionally the cabbage looper makes holes; remove damaged leaves and treat good foliage and immediate surroundings with iron phosphate slug bait or *Bacillus thuringiensis* for loopers. The plant can sucker from deep, thick woody roots, but they are easy to pull and remove where not wanted. Propagate from seed or root cuttings. USDA hardiness zones 4–8.

LANDSCAPE USE

The large leaves of curly leaf sea kale provide a focal point with a presence unlike any other herbaceous perennial. It looks good with just about any plant with similar cultural needs, adding contrast wherever planted. Best placed in the foreground and at corners or bends, it is a strong unifier when repeated in a composition as it draws the eye. Pair it with winecups, Cashmere sage, regal torchlily, UNDAUNTED ruby muhly, or SPANISH GOLD broom. Use it to offset the midsized textures of many perennials, or among grasses and subshrubs such as santolina and lavender. Attracts bees. Deer resistant.

NATIVE RANGE AND ORIGIN

Native to coastal northern Europe and around the Baltic and Black Seas, this species was grown from seed brought from England by plantswoman Lauren Springer Ogden in 1989 and popularized as a hardy ornamental in her 1994 book *The Undaunted Garden*. Nurseryman Kelly Grummons pioneered its commercial production in the Rocky Mountain region.

Dianthus

FIRST LOVE dianthus   ●   Caryophyllaceae (pink family)

SIZE ▶ 15–20 in. tall, 12–15 in. wide

FLOWERS ▶ shades of pink to white, late spring through fall

BEST FEATURES ▶ intensely fragrant, bright flowers turn from white to pink and deep rose; long-blooming

This landscape-worthy dianthus has so many unique traits: the flowers that range from deep rose red to white in the same cluster, and the stalwart upright habit (making them worthy of cutting for flowers) combine to make this an outstanding plant for either bedding in a mass, or spotting in the perennial border or xeriscape. Dianthus are one of the most drought tolerant, resilient perennials for western gardens, and this is one of the most distinctive in the genus.

CULTURE

Best in full sun but tolerates partial shade if given morning sun. Prefers well-drained, rich loam, but will grow in most soils, provided they are not too wet. Moderate watering to dry.

Propagate seed obtained from a proprietary breeding program; does not come true from garden-collected seed. USDA hardiness zones 3b–9.

LANDSCAPE USE

Often grown as an annual, FIRST LOVE dianthus provides a long season of color, but can persist several years in most regions given a good site. It makes for a unique element in annual bedding schemes and is stunning in massed plantings. It is also a striking element in a wild garden or perennial border. Put it near a path so you can smell the spicy scent of the flowers. Because FIRST LOVE dianthus blooms nearly all season long, it combines nicely with other medium to smaller rosy red-, blue-, purple-, and silver-leaved perennials such as the Mexicali penstemons, Grand Mesa penstemon, LITTLE TRUDY catmint, and sun daisies. Attracts bees, butterflies, and moths; an excellent nectar source.

NATIVE RANGE AND ORIGIN

This hybrid of Eurasian origin was developed by Akio Ito, a renowned plant breeder of Japanese-based Takii Seed Company.

Diascia integerrima 'P009S'

CORAL CANYON twinspur • Scrophulariaceae (figwort family)

SIZE ▷ 12–18 in. tall, 10–15 in. wide

FLOWERS ▷ coral-pink, early summer through fall

BEST FEATURES ▷ brightly colored coral flowers; long-blooming; very xeric

CORAL CANYON was the first of its kind since most twinspurs available at garden centers are not cold hardy and are sold as annuals. Particularly compact and long-blooming, CORAL CANYON is perhaps one of the best hardy plant introductions to ever come from South Africa.

CULTURE

Full sun to partial shade. Well-drained loam or sandy soil. Moderate watering to xeric. Heaviest blooms are in early summer and then again in late summer to fall. When the first flush of blooms is waning, shear or trim old flower stalks back to healthy leaves to encourage a lush second flowering season.

Be sure to plant in well-drained soil for best performance and longevity. Propagate by cuttings or plant divisions. USDA hardiness zones 4b–8.

LANDSCAPE USE

CORAL CANYON twinspur makes a great border perennial in dry gardens or xeriscapes. It can also be used in containers because of the long bloom time. Purple-leaved plants are excellent garden companions, complementing the dark "eye" of the coral blooms, such as Hopley's Purple oregano (*Origanum laevigatum*), Royal Purple smoke bush (*Cotinus coggygria*), Concorde or Helmond Pillar barberry (*Berberis thunbergii*), purple-leaved sedums, and hens and chicks (*Sempervivum*). Silver-foliaged plants also combine well; try Sea Foam sage, Turquoise Tails blue sedum, filigree daisy, and partridge feather. Attracts bees and butterflies.

NATIVE RANGE AND ORIGIN

The species is native to South Africa, often on high cliffs, but the selection was discovered in 1996 by Panayoti Kelaidis and introduced through Plant Select in 2000.

Digitalis obscura

SUNSET foxglove • Plantaginaceae (plantain family)

SIZE ▶ 14–24 in. tall, 15–20 in. wide

FLOWERS ▶ burnt sienna, summer

BEST FEATURES ▶ distinctively colored flowers; evergreen foliage for year-long interest; very tolerant of drought and alkaline soil

The trumpet-shaped flowers are burnt sienna suffused with bright gold and reddish highlights. The plant flowers profusely from early to midsummer, with scattered blooms sometimes appearing up to first frost. This unusual perennial performs particularly well in sunny, dry gardens.

CULTURE
Full sun to partial shade. Well-drained clay, loam, or sandy soil. Moderate watering to dry. Responds well to judicious shearing in spring before new growth begins. Deadhead to prolong bloom. The foliage can sunburn if grown in extremely exposed sites. Propagate by stem cuttings or by seeds. USDA hardiness zones 4b–9.

LANDSCAPE USE
SUNSET foxglove is nice as a border perennial and is also good in rock gardens. The plant's habit is somewhat shrubby, producing basal rosettes of substantial, almost waxy dark green willowy leaves with branching, upright flower stems. Combinations with purple-foliaged plants help to draw out the dark burgundy in the flowers' throats. TANAGER gazania, COLORADO GOLD gazania, and Blonde Ambition blue grama grass are excellent companions as well. Attracts bees. Deer resistant.

NATIVE RANGE AND ORIGIN
This is a rare species in central, eastern, and southern Spain to northern Morocco, on limestone in high mountain areas. The great British collectors Jim and Jenny Archibald introduced it in the early 1980s from a collection they made in Andalucía, Spain. Seeds from their collection quickly produced vigorous clumps at Denver Botanic Gardens.

Digitalis thapsi

SPANISH PEAKS foxglove • Scrophulariaceae (figwort family)

SIZE ▸ 12–18 in. tall, 10–12 in. wide

FLOWERS ▸ rose pink, early summer

BEST FEATURES ▸ bright rose-pink flowers; beautiful foliage all growing season; thrives in a variety of sites, especially dry shade

One of the greatest cries among gardeners is for plants that love dry shade, and few plants fit the bill better than this lovely foxglove. It makes compact mats of wonderfully furry rosettes. The 18-in. tall stems produce a succession of rose red flowers in early summer. Unlike the common foxglove, this selection is a long-lived perennial that will thrive in very dry conditions once established.

CULTURE
Full sun to full shade. Clay, loam, or sandy soil. Moderate watering to dry. Very carefree. Cut flowering stems back after bloom, or if you need seed, once the seed has ripened. Very insect and disease resistant, long-lived, and low maintenance. Propagate by seed, which is prodigious and easy to germinate, especially if you have a greenhouse or propagation frame. Larger old plants can be divided, or rosettes rooted by cutting. USDA hardiness zones 4b–9.

LANDSCAPE USE
SPANISH PEAKS foxglove can be quite long-lived in gardens and should be used in shady borders or woodlands. Although the flowers may last only three weeks, the mat of gorgeous, velvety foliage can make a beautiful small-scale groundcover in shady spots. Combine it with other plants that prefer full to partial shade, such as silky rock jasmine, mock bearberry manzanita, Carol Mackie daphne, or Avalanche white sun daisy. Attracts bees, butterflies, and moths; an excellent nectar source. Deer resistant.

NATIVE RANGE AND ORIGIN
The species is native to south-central Spain west to eastern Portugal. Jim and Jenny Archibald collected SPANISH PEAKS in southern Iberia.

Echinacea tennesseensis

Tennessee purple coneflower • Asteraceae (aster family)

SIZE ▶ 18–24 in. tall, 15–18 in. wide

FLOWERS ▶ pink, in summer

BEST FEATURES ▶ long-blooming; easy to grow; tolerates hot, dry sites

Wild Tennessee purple coneflower is found in Eastern red cedar (*Juniperus virginiana*) glades around Nashville, Tennessee. These openings in the forest develop where limestone bedrock close to the surface renders the soil too shallow for woody tree roots. Glades tend to be wetter in the winter and spring, then quite dry throughout the summer. Tennessee purple coneflower once thrived in them because its taproot could work its way through fissures in the limestone to access deeply seated moisture, a feature which makes it amazingly adaptable to drier, western gardens. Unfortunately, the rapid expansion and development of the Nashville area and its suburbs in the mid- to late twentieth century became an immediate threat to this habitat. After this species was added to the Endangered Species list in 1979, only the second plant to be added, public, private, state, and federal entities created and implemented a conservation plan where the existing coneflower populations were supplemented and protected. The threats were eventually neutralized and in 2011 the species was removed from the list. Inclusion in the Plant Select roster celebrates this official, federal recovery.

CULTURE

Full sun to partial shade. Clay, loam, or sandy soil. Moderate watering to dry. Flowers always face east so site accordingly. Deadhead to improve the appearance, or leave the spent blooms for the birds who love the seed heads. Very drought tolerant once established. Propagate by seeds, which need a 14-day cold moist stratification followed by 70°F days and 55°F nights. USDA hardiness zones 5–7.

LANDSCAPE USE

Tennessee purple coneflower works well in a perennial border, a wildflower garden, or an informal planting. Wonderful combinations with this coneflower include moon carrot, Wild Thing autumn sage, SUNSET foxglove, SONORAN SUNSET hyssop, winecups, and grasses such as Blonde Ambition blue grama grass and Korean feather reed grass. Attracts butterflies and bees. Deer resistant.

NATIVE RANGE AND ORIGIN

Tennessee purple coneflower is endemic to limestone cedar glades within a 14-mile radius covering three counties in the Nashville, Tennessee, area.

Echium amoenum

Red feathers ● Boraginaceae (borage family)

SIZE ▶ 10–16 in. tall, 6–8 in. wide

FLOWERS ▶ red, spring through summer

BEST FEATURES ▶ upright plumes covered in feathery, cherry-red flowers that fade to paler shades of pink and purple as they mature; adaptable to a variety of soils as well as moisture levels

Red feathers is an unusual perennial that provides a spiky, architectural quality in the garden. It consists of a basal tuft of dark green, bristly, linear leaves about 8 in. across from which emerge spikes of feathery, cherry-red flowers in spring.

CULTURE

Full sun to partial shade. Clay, loam, or sandy soil. Moderate watering to xeric. Deadhead for repeat bloom later in summer and fall, but leave some flower spikes to go to seed to ensure that this sometimes short-lived perennial persists in your garden. Drier conditions minimize excessive reseeding. All aboveground parts of red feathers are covered with fine, bristly hairs which can be irritating to the skin—be sure to wear gloves when handling. Propagate by seed, which germinates in 10–15 days; fluctuation in day and night temperatures may result in more consistent germination. USDA hardiness zones 3–9.

LANDSCAPE USE

Red feathers works well in dry to xeric gardens and rock gardens as well as in more moisture-loving perennial borders. Excellent garden companions include Sea Foam sage, LITTLE TRUDY catmint, and PLATINUM sage. Attracts bees, butterflies, and hummingbirds. Deer resistant.

NATIVE RANGE AND ORIGIN

Caucasus mountains in southwestern Russia and northern Iran.

Engelmannia peristenia

Engelmann's daisy • Asteraceae (aster family)

SIZE ▶ 24–28 in. tall, 14–18 in. wide

FLOWERS ▶ yellow, summer

BEST FEATURES ▶ bright yellow daisies throughout the summer; attractive mounds of wavy gray-green deeply cleft foliage; xeric

Engelmann's daisy delivers drifts of yellow daisies from early summer until fall, and its long taproot helps it access water even when rainfall is scarce. The petals fold downwards in intense heat and bright sunlight. Bees, butterflies, and hummingbirds visit the plants for nectar and pollen, and birds feed on the mature seeds.

CULTURE

Full sun to partial shade. Clay, loam, or sandy soil. Moderate watering to xeric. Very drought tolerant, but more floriferous when given supplemental water. Reblooms quickly after being cut back. Deadhead finished flower stalks to prevent the establishment of unwanted seedlings. Propagate by seed, which germinates well without pretreatment; cover seed lightly and maintain uniform moisture until seedlings are established. USDA hardiness zones 5–10.

LANDSCAPE USE

Use Engelmann's daisy in the perennial border, as a specimen plant, or in the xeriscape garden. It mixes well in wildflower plantings along with blanket flower (*Gaillardia grandiflora*), Narbonne blue flax, Tennessee purple coneflower, PRAIRIE JEWEL penstemon, Blonde Ambition blue grama, and UNDAUNTED ruby muhly grasses. Attracts bees, butterflies, and hummingbirds; an excellent nectar source. Deer resistant.

NATIVE RANGE AND ORIGIN

Great Plains from Missouri to Arizona and South Dakota to Texas. German-born physician and botanist George Engelmann first described this plant to science in the mid-1800s.

Epilobium fleischeri

Alpine willowherb • Onagraceae (evening primrose family)

SIZE ▶ 18–20 in. tall, 10–12 in. wide

FLOWERS ▶ pink, spring through summer

BEST FEATURES ▶ pink flowers nearly all season long; thrives in a wide range of soils, exposures, and habitats, xeric; compact and noninvasive; drought tolerant

Although alpine willowherb has been grown in European gardens for hundreds of years, it was virtually unknown in the United States. Denver Botanic Gardens acquired its seeds from Alpengarten Zenz (Graz-Grambach, Switzerland) in the 1908s. This diminutive, compact cousin of fireweed (*Epilobium angustifolium*) does not have its giant relative's weedy tendencies and is a true perennial. Finely textured gray-green foliage and wiry reddish stems provide the framework for delicate fuchsia-pink flowers that appear continuously from late spring into the fall. After the fruits dry, the "fluffy" seeds are carried away on the wind, providing yet another attractive trait that adds further interest as winter approaches.

CULTURE

Full sun to partial shade. Loam or sandy loam. Moderate watering. Susceptible to flea beetles. Cut damaged foliage back to promote new, healthy growth. It may reseed locally. Deadhead to limit reseeding. Propagate by seeds, which are very easy to germinate. Allow seedlings to dry thoroughly between waters; overwatering is the most common cause of seedling attrition. USDA hardiness zones 3–8.

LANDSCAPE USE

Alpine willowherb is excellent for massing and drifts in the foreground or middle of the perennial border, among rocks, in rock gardens, and in containers. It combines nicely with purple winter savory, MONGOLIAN BELLS clematis, and WIND-WALKER Garnet penstemon. Attracts bees.

NATIVE RANGE AND ORIGIN

Endemic to the Alps of central Europe.

Eriogonum wrightii var. *wrightii*

Snow Mesa buckwheat • Ericaceae (heath family)

SIZE ▶ 18–20 in. tall, 18–24 in. wide

FLOWERS ▶ white, summer

BEST FEATURES ▶ billowy clouds of white flowers that age to a rusty color late in the season

This plant has two very distinct growing phases. During most of the growing season it's a mat of silver foliage that makes an inviting carpet and attractive low accent. Later in the season it puts out long, wiry green flower-topped stems that explode with a mass of white blossoms attracting a multitude of bees and other beneficial insects.

CULTURE
Full sun. Clay, loam, or sandy soil. Dry to xeric. Requires very little maintenance. If the plant becomes rangy and unkempt in winter, cut it back to the mat of foliage and clean up the remaining duff. Propagate by seeds, which germinate well after a 14- to 30-day cold stratification; do not cover as seeds need light to germinate. USDA hardiness zones 4–9.

LANDSCAPE USE
Snow Mesa buckwheat is a great plant to put near the top of a dry stacked wall to allow the flowers to drape and cascade over. A late bloomer, it carries silvery basal foliage and pairs well with early- and midsummer xeric-blooming perennials such as SILVERTON bluemat and Coral Baby penstemons, red feathers, and Colorado desert blue star. Attracts bees. Deer resistant.

NATIVE RANGE AND ORIGIN
Western Slope of Colorado and all through the Colorado River Basin.

Erodium chrysanthum

Golden storksbill • Geraniaceae (geranium family)

SIZE ▶ 8–10 in. tall, 15–24 in. wide

FLOWERS ▶ creamy yellow, spring through late summer

BEST FEATURES ▶ buttery yellow flowers; lacey, silvery foliage; long season of bloom; long-lived; xeric

Few garden plants are as resilient yet beautiful as this unusual storksbill. Soft, silvery leaves combine well with most garden plants and are attractive nearly all year. The creamy yellow flowers add color for several months from spring through midsummer. The plant is as tough as nails, tolerating hail, wind, snow, sleet, and sun nearly unscathed. This species is also particularly adapted to dry conditions because of the thickened root structure that stores water, allowing the plant to survive extended periods of low precipitation without additional irrigation.

CULTURE
Full sun to partial shade. Well-drained loam or sandy soil. Moderate watering to xeric. The flowers are self-cleaning so little deadheading is needed. They're also sterile so plants don't seed around. The foliage is nearly evergreen; clean out old and dead leaves from the base and interior of the plant early in spring so that fresh, new leaves will fill in quickly. Propagate by tip cuttings. USDA hardiness zones 4–9.

LANDSCAPE USE
A long-lived, hardy, and adaptable perennial for edges of borders, rock gardens and xeriscapes, golden storksbill blooms heavily in early summer. Foliage is beautiful from early spring through late fall. Whether in or out of bloom, this lovely plant combines with a wide range of water-wise plants including red feathers, summer forget-me-not, PRAIRIE JEWEL penstemon, and LITTLE TRUDY catmint. Attracts bees, butterflies, and moths; an excellent nectar source. Deer resistant.

NATIVE RANGE AND ORIGIN
Northern Greece at higher altitudes in limestone scree and sandy soils.

Gazania linearis 'P004S'

COLORADO GOLD gazania • Asteraceae (aster family)

SIZE ▶ 4–6 in. tall, 10–12 in. wide

FLOWERS ▶ yellow, spring through fall

BEST FEATURES ▶ continuous large, showy yellow flowers on a compact, fire-resistant plant; good colonizer

Showy golden yellow flowers bloom almost continuously from late winter or early spring to frost over tufts of shiny grasslike foliage. Drought- and fire-resistant, COLORADO GOLD gazania thrives with little care.

CULTURE

Full sun to partial shade. Well-drained loam or sandy soil. Moderate watering to xeric. Thrives in heat with deep, infrequent watering and good drainage. Keep soil on the dry side to encourage more prolific blooming. Cut flower stems all the way back to the basal leaves when deadheading for a neater appearance. If spent flowers are left to form seeds they will spread profusely, a wonderful bonus for filling in open areas voluntarily. Deadhead on a regular basis to keep plant spread in check if so desired. Flowers open in sunlight so site accordingly. Propagate by seed, which needs no special treatment. Hardiness zone 4a–8.

LANDSCAPE USE

Use COLORADO GOLD gazania in beds, borders, and containers or as a groundcover. It is excellent for hot or sandy sites and pairs nicely with Turquoise Tails blue sedum, VALLEY LAVENDER plains verbena, hopflower oregano, the Mexicali penstemons, and Smoky Hills skullcap. Attracts butterflies, bees, bee-flies, ants, and beetles.

NATIVE RANGE AND ORIGIN

Gazania linearis is native to South Africa on rocky outcroppings and cliffs. The genus was named in honor of Theodore de Gaza, a fifteenth-century Greek scholar. Five centuries later, the strain COLORADO GOLD was selected for its vigor and cold hardiness by Panayoti Kelaidis of Denver Botanic Gardens.

Geranium magniflorum 'P013S'

LA VETA LACE geranium • Geraniaceae (geranium family)

SIZE ▶ 6–10 in. tall, 18–24 in. wide

FLOWERS ▶ purple, spring through summer

BEST FEATURES ▶ finely dissected foliage and large purple-lilac flowers; foliage in fall takes on scarlet and purple tints continuing into early winter

LA VETA LACE geranium has notable large flowers and distinctive lacey foliage that persists into the winter months when it turns scarlet and purple, providing wonderful tapestry-like texture.

CULTURE

Full sun to partial shade. Well-drained loam. Moderate watering to dry. Needs little maintenance other than light clean up in the spring. Propagate by seed, which should be covered lightly as light is not needed for germination. Also propagate by cuttings taken while the stems are still pink to reddish. USDA hardiness zones 4–8.

LANDSCAPE USE

LA VETA LACE geranium is striking when used in a mass or drift as a groundcover. It is suitable for rock gardens or at the front of a border, and does best on north- or east-facing slopes with moderate organic amendment in the soil for better moisture retention. This geranium is an attractive companion to spring bulbs and spring-flowering perennials such as oxlip primrose, LITTLE TRUDY catmint, and candytuft (*Iberis sempervirens*). Attracts bees.

NATIVE RANGE AND ORIGIN

Seed of *Geranium magniflorum*, which is native to central and eastern South Africa where it is common in moist grasslands to uplands, was collected by Panayoti Kelaidis, Denver Botanic Gardens, at the base of Joubert's Pass in the Drakensberg Mountains of Eastern Cape Province, in 1997. LA VETA LACE was selected from this germplasm.

Heuchera sanguinea 'Snow Angel'

Snow Angel coral bells • Saxifragaceae (saxifrage family)

SIZE ▸ 6 in. tall (12–15 in. in bloom), 8–12 in. wide

FLOWERS ▸ red, spring through summer

BEST FEATURES ▸ cream-and-green variegated foliage; performs well in dry shade

The low-growing mounds of light green, broadly lobed leaves are marbled with a light cream variegation that brightens any shady garden. Long-lasting panicles of bright pink-red bells appear on sturdy stems and float above the distinctive mound of foliage from late spring into summer. The species' name describes the blood red to carmine color of the flowers. This plant is adapted to monsoonal climates that have inconsistent wet seasons.

CULTURE
Partial sun to shade. Loam. Moderate watering; dry in shade. Remove faded flower stems to encourage formation of additional panicles. Propagate from stem cuttings to maintain consistent variegation. USDA hardiness zones 3–9.

LANDSCAPE USE
Snow Angel coral bells is a low, compact mounding perennial. It is attractive as an accent plant, in massing or in drifts. It's also an excellent plant for dry shade areas of the garden or the front to center of the border. Its showy foliage demands attention, so the best pairings are with more-subdued perennials, groundcovers, and shrubs such as mock bearberry manzanita, ice plants, MINI MAN dwarf Manchurian viburnum, and hopflower oregano. Attracts butterflies and hummingbirds. Deer resistant.

NATIVE RANGE AND ORIGIN
Harlan Hamernik of Bluebird Nursery in Clarkson, Nebraska, selected this unusual variegated form from a group of seedlings. The species is native from New Mexico to Arizona, into northern Mexico; in moist, shady rocky areas in mountains.

Monardella macrantha 'Marian Sampson'

Hummingbird trumpet mint • Lamiaceae (mint family)

SIZE ▸ 3–6 in. tall, 8–12 in. wide

FLOWERS ▸ red, spring through summer

BEST FEATURES ▸ brilliant red trumpet flowers through most of the season; shade tolerant

Marian Sampson is a showstopping rock garden plant, offering diverse garden application. The intensely aromatic fire-cracker red flowers are veritable hummingbird magnets whether the plant is in the ground, tumbling over a wall, or in a container. Marian Sampson was selected by Plant Select because of its remarkable adaptability and tolerance of afternoon shade, a great candidate for the ever-elusive dry shade area. It can be a short-lived perennial but makes up for it with its semiever-green foliage and showy floral display all summer long.

CULTURE
Partial sun. Clay, loam, or sandy soil. Moderate watering to dry. Requires very well-drained soil and is intolerant of frequent water. Needs moderate winter protection. Propagate by stem cuttings. USDA hardiness zones 5b–9.

LANDSCAPE USE
Hummingbird trumpet mint is a small perennial or ground-cover that can be planted individually for accent, in the rock garden, or xeriscape. It tolerates light shade, so it is a great candidate for a dry and somewhat shady area. The flame-red flowers are especially accented when paired with silver-leaved plants such as filigree daisy, partridge feather, Turquoise Tails blue sedum, and silverheels horehound. Attracts bees, butterflies, and hummingbirds; an excellent nectar source. Deer resistant.

NATIVE RANGE AND ORIGIN
The species is native to the higher mountain regions of southern California woodlands, forests and chaparral regions. The cultivar was originally selected by Ed Sampson of Mourning Cloak Ranch and Botanical Garden in Tehachapi, California, from seed collected in the Santa Rosa Mountains and named for his late wife, Marian, who was co-director of Mourning Cloak.

Nepeta 'Psfike'

LITTLE TRUDY catmint • Lamiaceae (mint family)

SIZE ▸ 8–15 in. tall, 12–15 in. wide

FLOWERS ▸ lavender-blue, spring through fall

BEST FEATURES ▸ compact growth habit; long season of bloom; xeric

Introduced by Plant Select in 2008, LITTLE TRUDY was one of the first dwarf catmints available. Everything about the plant is smaller—the overall stature, the flowers, and even the grayish-green serrated leaves. The extremely cold hardy plant will begin growing in very early spring.

CULTURE

Full sun to partial shade. Clay, loam, or sandy soil. Moderate watering to xeric. Unlike more vigorous forms of catmint, LITTLE TRUDY is sterile so does not produce seedlings in the garden. When the early summer flush of flowers has faded, either trim off old flower stalks down to a shapely mound of foliage, or allow plants to self-clean. Both methods seem to result in the same amount of rebloom later in the season. Cut plants back to emerging leaves in early spring. There are no known pest or disease issues, and the aromatic foliage keeps deer and rabbits from browsing. Propagate by cuttings. Commercial propagation of this patented plant is restricted to licensed growers. USDA hardiness zones 4–9.

LANDSCAPE USE

One of the most compact forms of catmint, LITTLE TRUDY can be used in mass plantings, to soften edges of borders, in rock gardens, and in containers. Suggested garden companions are Blonde Ambition blue grama grass, red feathers, golden storksbill, desert beardtongue, Bridges' penstemon, Wild Thing and Furman's Red autumn sages, and SUNSET foxglove. Attracts bees, butterflies, and moths; an excellent nectar source. Deer resistant.

NATIVE RANGE AND ORIGIN

This compact form was discovered by Brian Core, Little Valley Wholesale Nursery in Brighton, Colorado, and named for one of the founders of the nursery, Trudy Fike.

Oenothera macrocarpa subsp. *incana*

SILVER BLADE evening primrose • Onagraceae (evening primrose family)

SIZE ▶ 4–8 in. tall, 15–24 in. wide

FLOWERS ▶ yellow, late spring through summer

BEST FEATURES ▶ gleaming silver leaves; large lemon yellow flowers that are fragrant in the evening and at night; extremely long-blooming native; long-lived; easy care; more drought tolerant than the commonly grown green-leaved form of the species (subsp. *macrocarpa*).

Evening primroses are quintessential North American dry prairie and desert plants, with species found from Canada south into Texas. They have evolved to be tough, long-lived, long-blooming, and to save their flowers for the cooler, less windy parts of the day. To entice pollinators that come at dusk and later, the flower color must be luminescent and the blossom size large; alluring fragrance helps as well—all great qualities for a garden plant. SILVER BLADE has all of these qualities plus stunning waxy silver foliage.

CULTURE

Full sun. Loam. Moderate watering to xeric. Cut stems back to the base in late fall or late winter. Some years the plant is plagued by flea beetles that attack all members of the Onagraceae (evening primrose family). Douse afflicted foliage with topical pyrethrins when beetles are present but inactive early in the morning, avoiding flowers so as not to leave residue to harm pollinating insects arriving later. Propagate by seed or stem cuttings. USDA hardiness zones 4a–9.

LANDSCAPE USE

SILVER BLADE evening primrose's combination of silver and soft yellow shimmers in bright sunlight and glows in the evening. It is an ideal plant for evening gardens, softening hardscape, and edging xeric borders. The prostrate habit contrasts well with more upright xeric plants such as agastaches; red, purple, and blue penstemons; red yucca; blue salvias; and moon carrot. For prairie gardens, combine with Blonde Ambition blue grama or use as a loose groundcover with Sea Foam sage, ORANGE CARPET hummingbird trumpet, partridge feather, and manzanitas. Attracts hawkmoths, other moths, and bees. Deer resistant.

NATIVE RANGE AND ORIGIN

The species is native to southwestern Kansas and western Oklahoma into the Texas panhandle. The form sold as SILVER BLADE was collected in the wild and introduced by plantsman Jim Locklear. It was first commercially produced and promoted by Harlan Hamernik of Bluebird Nursery in Clarkson, Nebraska.

Origanum libanoticum

Hopflower oregano • Lamiaceae (mint family)

SIZE ▶ 10–15 in. tall, 18–24 in. wide

FLOWERS ▶ lavender-pink, summer through fall

BEST FEATURES ▶ long flowering season; for draping over walls or rocks for visual effect; attractive bluish gray-green foliage; good fresh cut flower; dried flower stems are ideal for floral arrangements

This extremely easy-to-grow plant adapts to a variety of settings. The main attraction is the hoplike bracts with delicate lavender-pink flowers that emerge from the chartreuse-toned bracts in early summer. The blooms rise on curving, wiry stems above a base of bluish-green foliage. The long season of interest—beginning in early spring and continuing through autumn—is notable.

CULTURE

Full sun to partial shade. Well-drained clay, loam, or sandy soil. Moderate watering to xeric. Produces abundant flowers to use as fresh cuts or to hang and dry for everlasting bouquets. Remaining flowers continue to be attractive in their senescence during the autumn. Remove old growth in late winter before new growth appears in the early spring. Propagate by stem cuttings which root easily when taken prior to the flowering stage. USDA hardiness zones 4–8.

LANDSCAPE USE

A wonderful accent in rock gardens, borders, planters, and mixed containers, hopflower oregano is very attractive when trailing or draping over walls or slopes where the interesting flower form shows off to great effect. This plant "plays well with others," including a wide array of perennials and grasses. A few suggestions include Smoky Hills skullcap; Mexicali and PRAIRIE JEWEL penstemons; and Blonde Ambition blue grama, UNDAUNTED ruby muhly, and Standing Ovation little bluestem grasses. Attracts bees and butterflies. Deer resistant.

NATIVE RANGE AND ORIGIN

Endemic in the northern Lebanon mountains in dry regions. Denver Botanic Gardens obtained seeds of the species from Carman's Nursery in Los Gatos, California, which had obtained seeds from J. H. Letswaart, author of the monograph of the genus. The species name refers to its homeland, Lebanon.

Osteospermum 'Avalanche'

Avalanche white sun daisy • Asteraceae (aster family)

SIZE ▶ 8–14 in. tall, 12–24+ in. wide

FLOWERS ▶ white daisies up to 3 in. wide, late spring to summer

BEST FEATURES ▶ long flowering period; cold hardiness; nearly evergreen, somewhat succulent leaves; xeric

Sun daisies (osteospermums) are typically annual plants, needing to be replanted each year, but Avalanche is the first cold-hardy white sun daisy to survive -25°F in Colorado trials. Flowering begins in late spring and continues through early summer, tapering off during the hottest part of summer. The bright white flowers are like a beacon inviting passersby or visitors to take notice.

CULTURE
Full sun to partial shade. Well-drained clay, loam, or sandy soil. Moderate watering to xeric. Propagate by cuttings. Commercial propagation of this patented plant is restricted to licensed growers. USDA hardiness zones 4–9.

LANDSCAPE USE
Flowers close up at dusk so be sure to site where they can be appreciated during the middle of the day. Plants spread vigorously, making a perfect edging for gardens, walkways, and at the top of rock walls. White mixes well with any color, and this low-spreading plant makes an attractive and useful filler in most types of gardens or landscapes. Attracts bees and butterflies.

NATIVE RANGE AND ORIGIN
Avalanche, likely a hybrid from unknown species native to the Drakensberg Mountains in South Africa, was selected from cultivated plants given to Denver Botanic Gardens by Austrian Fritz Kunert for superior cold hardiness and vigorous form. It also shows greater disease resistance and more abundant blooming than the other two osteospermums introduced by Plant Select.

Osteospermum barberiae var. compactum 'P005S'

PURPLE MOUNTAIN sun daisy • Asteraceae (aster family)

SIZE ▶ 12–14 in. tall and wide

FLOWERS ▶ purple daisies up to 3 in. wide, late spring through midsummer

BEST FEATURES ▶ long flowering period; cold hardiness

Bright purple daisylike flowers arise from compact, dense mats of evergreen foliage, obscuring the leaves in spring and blooming intermittently until autumn frosts.

CULTURE

Full sun to partial shade. Well-drained clay, loam, or sandy soil. Moderate watering to dry. Very particular about drainage, so be sure to avoid planting in low spots where moisture may persist for long periods. Deadhead to prolong blooming into later summer, but leave a few spent flowers to go to seed if desired. Propagate by cuttings. USDA hardiness zones 4b–9.

LANDSCAPE USE

The low-growing, spreading mounds are excellent for edging pathways and borders, in rock gardens, and in drifts. Flowers close up at dusk so site where the bright flowers can be enjoyed during the day. Combine with COLORADO GOLD gazania for a bright spring garden. Interplanting with any of the Mexicali penstemons will provide summer-long interest in a perennial garden. Attracts bees and butterflies.

NATIVE RANGE AND ORIGIN

The species is native to the summits of the Drakensberg Mountains in South Africa. This selection was chosen for cold hardiness, vigor, and abundant flowering.

Osteospermum 'P006S'

LAVENDER MIST sun daisy • Asteraceae (aster family)

SIZE ▶ 8–14 in. tall, 12–16 in. wide

FLOWERS ▶ large white daisies with dark eye aging to lavender, late spring through summer

BEST FEATURES ▶ long flowering period; cold hardiness; variation of flower colors on a single plant

Blooming through most of the summer, plants of LAVENDER MIST are often covered with both white and lavender flowers simultaneously—a most stunning effect. This pastel-colored daisy adds a cheerful look to landscapes and gardens in a wider range of gardens. Flowers are up to 3 in. across.

CULTURE
Full sun to partial shade. Well-drained clay, loam or sandy soil; plants are longer-lived in sites with excellent drainage. Moderate watering to dry. Old flowers can be removed to encourage longer flowering, but leave some to go to seed if volunteer seedlings are desired. Propagate by cuttings. USDA hardiness zones 4b–8.

LANDSCAPE USE
Use in drifts, in the foreground of garden borders, in rock gardens, in container plantings, and along walkways. The flowers close at night, so site accordingly. Combine with LITTLE TRUDY catmint, UNDAUNTED ruby muhly, and golden storksbill for summer-long color and interest. Attracts bees and butterflies.

NATIVE RANGE AND ORIGIN
This selection appears to be of hybrid origin because of its vigor and long blooming period. The genus is native to higher altitudes of South Africa's Drakensberg Mountains. Original plants were given to Denver Botanic Gardens by Blooming Nursery, Cornelius, Oregon.

Penstemon 'Coral Baby'

Coral Baby penstemon, Coral Baby beardtongue • Plantaginaceae (plantain family)

SIZE ▶ 15 in. tall and wide

FLOWERS ▶ coral-pink, spring through midsummer

BEST FEATURES ▶ upright spikes of bright, coral-pink flowers make it a magnet for hummingbirds; bright green foliage; long-lived

The bright green foliage is handsome and sets off the intensely saturated color of the flowers that appear from late spring into midsummer. Coral Baby is longer-lived than many penstemons, and the compact form and stunning flower display make this plant a perfect choice for many gardens.

CULTURE
Full sun. Sandy soil. Moderate watering to dry. Undemanding if planted in full sun and well-drained soil. Remove faded flower stems to promote reblooming. Propagate by tip cuttings taken from nonflowering shoots while plant is actively growing; cuttings root easily in 7–10 days in a 70°F greenhouse; reduce temperature and moisture as plants root in; keep blooms off to maintain a vegetative state for propagation. USDA hardiness zones 5–8.

LANDSCAPE USE
Coral Baby penstemon is beautiful in a dry border or rock garden and combines nicely with other xeric perennials, grasses, and shrubs. Its long-blooming nature adds color to water-wise gardens for many weeks. Plant it with Blonde Ambition blue grama grass, Smoky Hills skullcap, LITTLE TRUDY catmint, and golden storksbill. Attracts hummingbirds, bees, hawkmoths, and butterflies. Deer resistant.

NATIVE RANGE AND ORIGIN
Coral Baby penstemon appeared as a seedling from the cross between *Penstemon barbatus* 'Rondo' and *P. barbatus* 'Schooley's Yellow' and was brought to Plant Select by Kelly Grummons, Denver nurseryman and breeder specializing in xeric plants. The parent species is native to California, Arizona, and New Mexico.

Penstemon grandiflorus 'P010S'

PRAIRIE JEWEL penstemon, PRAIRIE JEWEL beardtongue • Plantaginaceae (plantain family)

SIZE ▸ 20–36 in. tall, 8–12 in. wide

FLOWERS ▸ a mix of purple and white, early summer

BEST FEATURES ▸ large cool-colored flowers; evergreen blue-gray foliage rosettes

PRAIRIE JEWEL strain is one of the most beautiful penstemons in cultivation today. The large 2-in. tubular flowers resemble inflated snapdragons and range in color from white to rose to lavender to burgundy. Arranged on tall, unbranched spires, the lovely flowers emerge from clasping eucalyptus-like rounded foliage that is beautiful in its own right. The combination is breathtaking in mass plantings.

CULTURE

Full sun. Dry loam or sandy loam; tolerates dry clay soil but won't grow as well. Dry to xeric. Avoid overwatering or plant will be short-lived; it will rot or not come through the winter. Cut back all but a couple of flowering stems before they set seed to prolong life but also allow for reseeding. Propagate by seed; cold-stratify for 30 days or soak for 4 hours in 500 ppm gibberellic acid. USDA hardiness zones 3–9.

LANDSCAPE USE

This plant, like most penstemons, resents competition, so don't crowd it except with itself. It is ideal in mass plantings, threaded through hellstrips, or in very open meadows. Combine it with partridge feather, Sea Foam sage, Narbonne blue flax, Lavender Ice ice plant, VALLEY LAVENDER plains verbena, or Blonde Ambition blue grama grass. Attracts bumblebees and honeybees. Deer resistant.

NATIVE RANGE AND ORIGIN

The wild species is native from Illinois to North Dakota and Wyoming, south to Texas. The name PRAIRIE JEWEL honors South Dakota rancher and plantsman Claude Barr, author of *Jewels of the Plains*, whose purportedly favorite plant was *Penstemon grandiflorus*. He collected seed from the Black Hills of South Dakota and shared it with Denver plantswoman Mary Ann Heacock in the early 1960s. Over a few decades of backcrossing and breeding in her garden with various other penstemons including *P. kunthii*, *P. parryi*, *P. murrayanaus*, and the Seeba strain, this colorful, vigorous strain was developed. Denver area nurseryman Kelly Grummons brought it to Plant Select.

Penstemon mensarum

Grand Mesa penstemon, Grand Mesa beardtongue • Plantaginaceae (plantain family)

SIZE ▶ 24–30 in. tall, 10–15 in. wide

FLOWERS ▶ blue, spring

BEST FEATURES ▶ brilliant cobalt blue flowers in a shade of blue rarely encountered in gardens; rosettes of evergreen foliage turn reddish orange in the fall; flowers strongly attract bees

United States Forest Service collector Arthur F. McDuffie collected the first specimen of *Penstemon mensarum* in 1912, and Francis W. Pennell, botanist at the New York Botanical Garden, published the first description of the plant in 1920. The species name *mensarum* means "of the table" (or mesa), in reference to the plant being found on the Grand Mesa in Colorado. Grand Mesa penstemon is not endangered in the wild, but the Colorado Natural Heritage Program has described it as "imperiled" because it's endemic to only three counties in western Colorado. Fortunately, commercial seed producers have been able to supply seed to the nursery industry so it is not necessary to collect seed from the limited native populations.

CULTURE

Full sun to partial shade. Clay, loam, or sandy soil. Moderate watering to xeric. Cutting back spent flower spikes before they start to set seed allows the plants to store more carbohydrates for a stronger floral display in the following spring. Propagate by seeds, which require a minimum of 30 days of cold/moist stratification; cover seed lightly and maintain uniform moisture until seedlings are established. Also propagate by basal stem cuttings treated with a moderate dose of rooting hormones and placed under intermittent mist; roots from in 8–10 days. USDA hardiness zones 3–9

LANDSCAPE USE

Adaptable to a wide range of garden conditions, Grand Mesa penstemon can be used in a perennial border, rock garden, or xeriscape garden. As an early bloomer, it combines with SILVER BLADE evening primrose, COLORADO GOLD or TANAGER gazania, and partridge feather. Attracts bees. Deer resistant.

NATIVE RANGE AND ORIGIN

Endemic to western Colorado.

Penstemon ×mexicali 'Carolyn's Hope'

Carolyn's Hope penstemon ● Plantaginaceae (plantain family)

SIZE ▶ 14–18 in. tall, 12–14 in. wide

FLOWERS ▶ pink, throughout much of the summer

BEST FEATURES ▶ pink with darker buds; long season of bloom; adaptable to a wide range of garden conditions

Some pink flowers are too pale to hold up in the bright sunshine of higher-altitude gardens, but this form is bold and clear, and the dark buds add a beautiful contrast to the dark glossy green foliage. Easy to grow and blooms nearly all summer long if deadheaded.

CULTURE
Full sun, partial shade. Clay, loam, or sandy soil. Moderate watering to dry. Remove spent flowers to encourage continual blooming. Cut plants to ground in spring for full, new growth. Propagate by cuttings. USDA hardiness zones 4b–8.

LANDSCAPE USE
Ideal for planting in masses, or mixed in perennial borders, habitat gardens, rock gardens, or meadow gardens. Pair with smaller ornamental grasses such as Standing Ovation little bluestem and Blonde Ambition blue grama grass. Daisylike flowers such as Tennessee purple coneflower and Avalanche white sun daisy also make stunning perennial combinations. Attracts bees, bumblebees, moths, and butterflies. Deer resistant.

NATIVE RANGE AND ORIGIN
Carolyn's Hope was developed by Brian Core, Little Valley Wholesale Nursery, Brighton, Colorado, to honor his wife, Carolyn. Funds raised through sales of this plant benefit breast cancer research at University of Colorado Cancer Center.

Penstemon ×mexicali 'PO08S'

RED ROCKS penstemon • Plantaginaceae (plantain family)

SIZE ▶ 14–18 in. tall, 12–14 in. wide

FLOWERS ▶ reddish with a white throat, throughout much of the summer

BEST FEATURES ▶ rosy-red flowers; long season of bloom; adaptable to a wide range of garden conditions

RED ROCKS was one of the first of the hybrid Mexicali penstemons to come from the breeding work of Bruce Myers, and has since become a staple landscape plant in many parts of the country because of its stunning garden performance and hardiness.

CULTURE
Full sun, partial shade. Clay, loam, or sandy soil. Moderate watering to dry. Remove faded flowers to promote continued flowering. Often evergreen, wait until spring to cut back. Propagate by cuttings. USDA hardiness zones 4b–8.

LANDSCAPE USE
Useful in habitat gardens, perennial borders, rock gardens, and even large containers. Combine with wine cups, allowing the spreading native groundcover to intertwine around and between. Stunning when planted with bright white flowers such as Avalanche sun daisy, or with blue-flowered LITTLE TRUDY catmint or Narbonne flax. Attracts bees, bumblebees, moths, and butterflies. Deer resistant.

NATIVE RANGE AND ORIGIN
Selected by Ray Daugherty at Green Acres Nursery in Golden, Colorado, from plants grown from Bruce Meyers's seed. Bruce was an amateur hybridizer in White Salmon, Washington, who specialized in hybridizing various showy Mexican, nonhardy *Penstemon* species with cold-hardy American species. Plant Select has been rewarded many times over from the efforts of Bruce Meyers who, unfortunately, passed away before the introduction of these outstanding plants. His legacy is truly important to amateur plant hybridizers everywhere.

Penstemon ×mexicali 'Psmyers'

SHADOW MOUNTAIN penstemon • Plantaginaceae (plantain family)

SIZE ▸ 18–24 in. tall, 14–18 in. wide

FLOWERS ▸ lavender with a white throat, throughout much of the summer

BEST FEATURES ▸ lavender-blue flowers with strongly striped throat; long season of bloom; adaptable to a wide range of garden conditions

SHADOW MOUNTAIN is the tallest of the five Plant Select Mexicali penstemon selections, offering a narrower form but with the same ornamental features of glossy green narrow leaves and a long-blooming floriferous habit as the others. The lavender-blue flower color adds a soft grace to gardens.

CULTURE
Full sun, partial shade. Clay, loam, or sandy soil. Moderate watering to dry. Remove spent flowers to encourage longer blooming. Cut plants to ground in spring. Propagate by cuttings. USDA hardiness zones 4b–8.

LANDSCAPE USE
Excellent choice for perennial gardens, wildflower gardens, habitat gardens, and meadow gardens. Combine with smaller native grass selections such as Standing Ovation little bluestem and Blonde Ambition blue grama. Blue-flowered perennials such as LITTLE TRUDY catmint and Cape forget-me-not will enhance the blue tones of the flowers. Purple-flowered plants, such as PIKE'S PEAK PURPLE penstemon and PURPLE MOUNTAIN sun daisy, will bring out the lavender hues. Attracts bees, bumblebees, moths, and butterflies. Deer resistant.

NATIVE RANGE AND ORIGIN
SHADOW MOUNTAIN appeared as a variant of PIKE'S PEAK PURPLE at Welby Gardens Westwoods in Arvada, Colorado.

Penstemon ×mexicali 'PWIN02S'

WINDWALKER Garnet penstemon • Plantaginaceae (plantain family)

SIZE ▸ 14–18 in. tall, 12–14 in. wide

FLOWERS ▸ garnet with a white throat, throughout much of the summer

BEST FEATURES ▸ ruby-red flowers with striped throat; long season of bloom; adaptable to a wide range of garden conditions

Fifth in the series of hybrid Mexicali penstemons from Plant Select, WINDWALKER Garnet is the deepest-colored of them all. Glossy green foliage, almost evergreen, contrasts beautifully with the garnet-colored flowers. Plants bloom nearly all summer with adequate moisture and sun.

CULTURE
Full sun, partial shade. Clay, loam, or sandy soil. Moderate watering to dry. Deadhead to discourage seed production and to encourage continual blooming. Trim plants to ground in spring. Propagate by cuttings. USDA hardiness zones 4b–8.

LANDSCAPE USE
Useful in a wide range of gardens, but the dark flowers are best appreciated when seen up close or when contrasted with silvery-foliaged plants or perennials with white flowers. Silvery companions include baby blue rabbitbrush, silverheels horehound, and Sea Foam sage. The white flowers of Dalmatian daisy, Avalanche sun daisy, and silver sage offer bright backdrops for the jewel-toned flowers. Attracts bees, bumblebees, moths, butterflies. Deer resistant.

NATIVE RANGE AND ORIGIN
Developed by Kelly Grummons, Denver-area plantsman and breeder specializing in xeric plants.

Penstemon pseudospectabilis

Desert penstemon, desert beardtongue • Plantaginaceae (plantain family)

SIZE ▸ 36 in. tall, 20 in. wide

FLOWERS ▸ pink, spring through early summer

BEST FEATURES ▸ tubular hot pink flowers; xeric; long-lived

Showy flowers begin blooming in late spring, complemented by large, leathery upcurved leaves that take on a purple cast in late fall and often remain evergreen in mild winters. Native to the Southwest, this species thrives in sandy soil and hot xeric conditions. Hummingbirds are strongly attracted to the flowers and songbirds eat the seeds. The flowers are an important nectar and pollen source for native bees and honeybees.

CULTURE

Full sun to partial shade. Well-drained clay or sandy soil. Dry to xeric. Seed heads may be left on for winter interest and forage, or trimmed after flowering to prevent seedlings. A few deep soakings during the growing season will prolong bloom time. Propagate by seeds, which require cold stratification; fall planting is ideal; cover with a thin layer of soil. USDA hardiness zones 5–9.

LANDSCAPE USE

Desert penstemon is a tough and beautifully bright plant for difficult areas with little irrigation. It makes a majestic addition to rock gardens or borders. Heat-loving perennials such as Narbonne blue flax, Sunset hyssop, summer forget-me-not, red yucca, chocolate flower, and winecups are perfect garden partners. Attracts hummingbirds, sphinx moths, and bees. Deer resistant.

NATIVE RANGE AND ORIGIN

California, Arizona, New Mexico, Utah.

Penstemon rostriflorus

Bridges' penstemon, Bridges' beardtongue • Syn. *Penstemon bridgesii*

Plantaginaceae (plantain family)

SIZE ▶ 24–36 in. tall and wide

FLOWERS ▶ red, summer

BEST FEATURES ▶ bright red tubular flowers; great for attracting hummingbirds; tolerates a wide range of soil types and sites; xeric

Bridges' penstemon is a wonderful addition to the dry western landscape. The glossy foliage is attractive and turns shades of red and bronze throughout the winter. This penstemon blooms later than most of the rest of the genus, making it a season extender for the xeriscape. The later bloom period also provides an important nectar source for hummingbirds and pollinators, helping them survive through the long dry summer months when many other cool-season plants have shut down for the summer.

CULTURE

Full sun to partial shade. Clay, loam or sandy soil. Moderate watering to xeric. Deadhead as flower spikes age and plants will continue to send up new flower spikes throughout the season. Propagate by seed, which germinates well after a 45-day cold stratification. USDA hardiness zones 4b–8.

LANDSCAPE USE

Bridges' penstemon is a great addition to the prairie or steppe garden and gives a very naturalistic feel when planted among grasses. It forms an attractive, somewhat shrubby mound of 2- to 3-foot-tall stems with linear green foliage. It also makes a good scrambling perennial for the rock garden or more traditional xeriscape. This late-summer bloomer combines nicely with Blonde Ambition blue grama and Standing Ovation little bluestem grasses, Mojave sage, Gold on Blue prairie zinnia, and baby blue rabbitbrush. Attracts bees, butterflies, and moths; an excellent nectar source. Deer resistant.

NATIVE RANGE AND ORIGIN

Eastern slope of the Greater Sierra Nevada range and throughout the Great Basin.

Phlomis cashmeriana

Cashmere sage • Lamiaceae (mint family)

SIZE ▶ 36–60 in. tall, 18–30 in. wide

FLOWERS ▶ lavender, summer

BEST FEATURES ▶ a large perennial for challenging sites; tolerates dry shade; in autumn, tall inflorescences leave an interesting whorled stalk for winter interest or dried arrangements

The genus *Phlomis* consists of dozens of species that grow throughout Eurasia. Most of them have flowers in the lavender tones, some are annuals, and others grow at alpine elevations, but none seem to have the garden appeal and versatility of *P. cashmeriana*.

CULTURE

Full sun to partial shade. Clay, loam, or sandy soil. Moderate watering to dry. Remove dead stalks and debris in early spring or late winter before the plants are actively growing. Let the inflorescences stand through the winter to add interest and texture to the winter landscape. Propagate by seeds, which are large and germinate best with soil temperatures above 70°F. USDA hardiness zones 4b–8.

LANDSCAPE USE

Cashmere sage is a large and stately perennial that blends comfortably in the traditional garden border and is well suited to mass plantings in a large space that needs to be filled. It does well in tough or neglected areas that can be hard to irrigate or where regular access is difficult during the growing season. Because it is large statured, it pairs agreeably with bold plants such as moon carrot, WINDWALKER big bluestem, giant sacaton, curly leaf sea kale, fernbush, and Apache plume. Attracts bees and bumblebees. Deer resistant.

NATIVE RANGE AND ORIGIN

Asia in the greater Himalaya complex.

Salvia argentea

Silver sage • Lamiaceae (mint family)

SIZE ▸ 6–8 in. tall (24–36 in. in bloom), 18–24 in. wide

FLOWERS ▸ white, summer

BEST FEATURES ▸ large felted, silvery leaves with wavy margins; showy white flowers in "candelabras" for a short period in early summer

Silver sage has been in cultivation for 100 years or more, but it was not sold in the United States until the 1990s when Plant Select recommended it. At that time, the plant had been grown by a number of gardeners along the Colorado Front Range and showcased by Panayoti Kelaidis in a stunning simple grouping with pink rock soapwort in Denver Botanic Gardens' Rock Alpine Garden in the late 1980s and early 1990s. It is considered a biennial in maritime regions, but has proven to be a long-lived perennial in dry regions.

CULTURE

Full sun to partial shade. Well-drained clay, loam, or sandy soil. Moderate watering to xeric. Cut flowers back as soon as they're finished to help refresh the beautiful foliage. Plants prefer dry to xeric conditions. Do not overwater if you want it to live long and prosper. Overhead watering rots the foliage. Propagate by seed, which needs light to germinate. USDA hardiness zones 4a–10.

LANDSCAPE USE

Silver sage is an excellent accent plant as both foliage and flowers draw the eye. Small groupings are most effective; use it in dry cottage gardens and casual borders. It is a nice foreground plant for medium-sized shrubs such as Apache plume, bluestem joint fir, and SPANISH GOLD broom. In a hellstrip, thread it through winecups, ice plants, or VALLEY LAVENDER plains verbena for high contrast and simplicity. Elsewhere, combine it with rose or pink penstemons, *Salvia greggii* selections, Mojave sage, moon carrot, agastaches, chocolate flower, or Narbonne blue flax. Attracts bees. Deer resistant.

NATIVE RANGE AND ORIGIN

The species is native from southern Europe to northwestern Africa and eastern Mediterranean. Avid Denver area gardener Mrs. J. V. "Pete" Petersen provided the original seed for Plant Select, and Bluebird Nursery, Clarkson, Nebraska, began commercially producing the plant.

Salvia daghestanica

PLATINUM sage • Lamiaceae (mint family)

SIZE ▶ 8–10 in. tall, 12–18 in. wide

FLOWERS ▶ blue, early summer

BEST FEATURES ▶ silvery white foliage; spikes of blue flowers; xeric

PLATINUM sage practically glimmers with frosty silvery leaves topped with spikes of electric dark blue flowers in whorls up the stem through the spring and early summer. Once the flowers are faded the foliage loosely resembles a miniature dusty miller even into early winter. PLATINUM sage may spread from seed though not in an aggressive fashion, creating tiny clumps. Sometimes small plantlets will form on the spikes after the flowers fade, the weight of them bending the stem to the ground where the plantlet may take root.

CULTURE
Full sun to partial shade. Loam or sandy soil. Dry to xeric. Deadhead spent flowers to encourage sporadic rebloom. Be sure to plant it in well-drained soil. Wait until new growth appears in spring before cleaning out dead-looking leaves. Propagate by seed or cuttings. USDA hardiness zones 5–10.

LANDSCAPE USE
Its compact habit and xeric tendencies make PLATINUM sage a perfect plant for tucking into small spaces among the cracks and crevices of rock gardens, or it can be used as a small specimen in hot, dry borders. It makes a stunning combination with COLORADO GOLD gazania, SILVER BLADE evening primrose, or FIRE SPINNER ice plant. Attracts bees. Deer resistant.

NATIVE RANGE AND ORIGIN
Russia, North Caucasus Mountains.

Salvia pachyphylla

Mojave sage • Lamiaceae (mint family)

SIZE ▸ 18–24 in. tall, 24–30 in. wide

FLOWERS ▸ lavender-blue, mid- to late summer

BEST FEATURES ▸ long flowering season; striking flower colors of lavender-blue and purple; very drought tolerant

The beautiful silvery green foliage is covered densely with short, soft hairs and is intensely aromatic. The flowers are violet-blue and appear on spikes of densely whorled bracts that are a smoky mauve purple. Late in the season flower color fades to brown and adds a subtle contrast to the semievergreen foliage that continues to add winter interest in the garden.

CULTURE

Full sun. Well-drained loam or sandy soil. Dry to xeric. Established plants do not need additional irrigation. Provide excellent drainage for winter moisture to drain away from the root system; poor drainage in winter will severely damage the plant. Prune in spring to remove damaged or unattractive stems, to reduce plant size, or to shape the plant. Woody stems will develop and it's best to prune to where new leaflets or branches are emerging. Propagate by seed, which may germinate faster if presoaked; seed will also germinate if kept wet. Also propagate by cuttings; use a talc-based rooting hormone. USDA hardiness zones 5–10.

LANDSCAPE USE

Mojave sage is a striking plant in xeric gardens, either as a specimen accent or in small groups or drifts where the shrublike form and attractive foliage provide background and contrast with other dryland plants. The silver-foliage and deep purple-lavender flowers combine well with Bridges' penstemon, hopflower oregano, LITTLE TRUDY catmint, and baby blue rabbitbrush. Attracts butterflies and hummingbirds. Deer resistant.

NATIVE RANGE AND ORIGIN

Nevada, northern Arizona, Southern California, and Baja California. Denver Botanic Gardens acquired seeds of this plant from Alplains in Kiowa, Colorado, whose proprietor originally collected the seeds in the Kingston Mountains of California.

Salvia reptans 'P016S'

Autumn Sapphire sage • Lamiaceae (mint family)

SIZE ▶ 18–24 in. tall and wide

FLOWERS ▶ blue, fall

BEST FEATURES ▶ late-season color; blue flowers; willowy appearance; xeric

Low maintenance is the mantra of this wonderful perennial selected for its clouds of sapphire blue flowers in autumn, when other flowers have faded. It also has a compact and consistent growth habit.

CULTURE
Full sun to partial shade. Clay, loam, or sandy soil. Dry to xeric. Low maintenance. Cut plants back to the ground in midspring when new growth begins to show. Propagate by cuttings or divisions only. USDA hardiness zones 5–10.

LANDSCAPE USE
AUTUMN SAPPHIRE sage mixes nicely in meadow gardens, xeriscapes, and especially in gardens designed for attracting pollinators. It pairs well with other late-season bloomers such as ORANGE CARPET hummingbird trumpet, Gold on Blue prairie zinnia, and UNDAUNTED ruby muhly. Attracts bees, butterflies, moths, and hummingbirds; excellent pollen and nectar source for late-season pollinators. Deer resistant.

NATIVE RANGE AND ORIGIN
Native to West Texas higher elevations (steppe areas), Texas grass sage (*Salvia reptans*) was brought to the attention of Plant Select by Lauren Springer Ogden and several gardeners of the Denver Botanic Gardens. Seeds of the hardiest plants were collected and grown on in the trial gardens at Colorado State University in Fort Collins and at the Denver Botanic Gardens Chatfield Farms. Among the variable seed-grown plants two selections were narrowed down for a second round of evaluations. One of these, AUTUMN SAPPHIRE sage, is the culmination of many years of evaluation and rigorous selection to bring to market a plant that blooms well at the end of the season and has all the best qualities that Texas grass sage has to offer.

Satureja montana var. *illyrica*

Purple winter savory • Syn. *Satureja subspicata* subsp. *subspicata* • Lamiaceae (mint family)

SIZE ▶ 4–6 in. tall, 12–15 in. wide

FLOWERS ▶ violet-lavender, late summer through fall

BEST FEATURES ▶ nearly evergreen, low-growing herb that is adaptable to a wide range of conditions; showy flowers late in the season

This is a compact, violet-lavender flowered form of the popular garden herb. Leafing out early in spring, it maintains a dark green color throughout summer and late into the fall when many other perennials are looking tired. This form is not recommended for culinary use as the flavor of the leaves is bitter. It is excellent for attracting bees and sphinx moths that fly in early evening.

CULTURE

Full sun to partial shade, Well-drained clay, loam, or sandy soil. Moderate watering to xeric. Very low maintenance. Cut plants back to the ground in early spring when new growth emerges. Not susceptible to pests or diseases. Propagate by seed, which can be scattered over the surface—do not cover. Also propagate by division. USDA hardiness zones 3b–8.

LANDSCAPE USE

Purple winter savory is a rich green, low-growing plant for the front of garden borders, rock gardens, or small spaces. It can also be used in containers. This unassuming little perennial combines well with a wide range of smaller-scale perennials, including the Mexicali penstemons, dwarf beach-head iris, Dalmatian pink cranesbill, and Corsican violet. Attracts bees and moths. Deer resistant.

NATIVE RANGE AND ORIGIN

High elevations from southern Europe to northern Africa, often on rocky slopes.

Scutellaria resinosa 'Smoky Hills'

Smoky Hills skullcap • Lamiaceae (mint family)

SIZE ▶ 8–10 in. tall, 10–14 in. wide

FLOWERS ▶ blue, summer

BEST FEATURES ▶ tidy growth habit; tolerates drought and heat; bright purple-blue flowers

This sturdy little beauty meets all of the criteria Plant Select demands of selections and was originally promoted by the GREAT PLANTS FOR THE GREAT PLAINS program. The durability and resilience of this charming plant that grows in neat mounds and covers itself with purple-blue flowers tipped with white markings through the summer makes it a perfect choice for gardeners in search of plants that require little water once established.

CULTURE

Full sun. Loam or sandy soil. Dry to xeric. Deadhead occasionally to encourage repeat flowering through the summer and early fall. Propagate by cuttings, which root best from tips and should be about 2 in. long; disbud any potential flower parts; can be rooted any time plants are in active growth. USDA hardiness zones 4–9.

LANDSCAPE USE

The tidy habit makes Smoky Hills blue skullcap perfect for a rock garden or a trough, as well as in the front of a border. The bright purple-blue flowers are wonderful in combination with small, yellow-flowering perennials such as chocolate flower, Gold on Blue prairie zinnia, or Goldhill golden-aster. Attracts bees. Deer resistant.

NATIVE RANGE AND ORIGIN

Smoky Hills blue skullcap comes from the short grass prairie habitat of the Smoky Hills of north-central Kansas.

Seseli gummiferum

Moon carrot • Apiaceae (carrot family)

SIZE ▶ 24–30 in. tall, 10–15 in. wide

FLOWERS ▶ pink fading to white, midsummer through fall

BEST FEATURES ▶ easy to grow in either full sun or partial shade; not fussy about soil; adaptable to a wide range of conditions

The species name is derived from the Latin word for *gum*, referring to the yellowish, aromatic resin exuded by the flowering stalks. The common name of this species evokes an image that is hard to resist. The silvery blue, lacy foliage is densely covered with short, soft hairs. A substantial flower stalk is produced the second year, bearing many pale pink, fading to white, flowers clustered in large, flat umbels. Blooms are continuous and generous from midsummer through fall.

CULTURE

Full sun to partial shade. Clay, loam, or sandy soil. Moderate watering to xeric. Usually treated as a biennial (forming a basal rosette the first year, blooming and setting seed, then dying out the second year). Allow the plant to produce seeds, then harvest or allow it to self-sow for future garden displays. Reseeding may be locally abundant and seedlings may require thinning. Propagate by seeds, which germinate readily without pretreatment. USDA hardiness zones 5–9.

LANDSCAPE USE

Moon carrot is striking as an architectural accent, in mixed dry borders, in containers and planters, and in dry rock gardens. Try planting it with Denver Daisy black-eyed Susan, Tennessee purple coneflower, or Ruby Voodoo rose. Its lacy foliage and stunning flowers add grace and beauty to a variety of midsized perennials and flowering shrubs. Pollinators: bees; an excellent plant for attracting beneficial insects such as lady bird beetles and flower flies. Deer resistant.

NATIVE RANGE AND ORIGIN

South Aegean region and into Bulgaria, on limestone cliffs. Denver Botanic Gardens acquired the original seed lot of this species from a botanical garden in Europe.

Tanacetum cinerariifolium

Dalmatian daisy • Asteraceae (aster family)

SIZE ▶ 15–20 in. tall, 18–24 in. wide

FLOWERS ▶ white daisylike with a yellow center, summer

BEST FEATURES ▶ gray-green cleft foliage in a casual rosette; airy-stemmed pure white flowers; pest- and browse-free; moderately long-lived; mildly self-sowing but not invasive like ox-eye daisy; tolerates dry conditions

Daisies are ever popular, and with ox-eye daisy (*Leucanthemum vulgare*) invasive at higher elevations and thirsty Shasta daisy (*L. ×superbum*) also sometimes invasive in moist areas, this drought-tolerant, mildly self-seeding natural source of the insecticide pyrethrin fills the bill for white daisies in the western garden.

CULTURE

Full sun to partial shade. Well-drained clay, loam, or sandy soil. Moderate watering to dry. Cut back finished flower stalks in midsummer to refresh the appearance and to minimize seeding if not desired. Cut back winter-damaged old foliage around the edge of the rosette in late winter to make room for new spring growth. Propagate by seeds; no pretreatment necessary. USDA hardiness zones 4–10.

LANDSCAPE USE

Dalmatian daisy is a cheerful addition to a sunny dry garden, with a casual, cottagey demeanor. Pure white daisies shimmer in bright sun as well as in low light in the evening, creating a cool ambiance among more brightly colored flowers. This dependable daisy combines especially well with penstemons, KANNAH CREEK buckwheat, Smoky Hills blue skullcap, Narbonne blue flax, Scott's sugarbowls, SILVER BLADE evening primrose, and Blonde Ambition blue grama grass. Deer resistant.

NATIVE RANGE AND ORIGIN

Balkans, Albania. It was long grown by herbalists but not trialed for cold hardiness and ornamental value until the late 1990s and early 2000s by curator Dan Johnson and plantswoman Lauren Springer Ogden in Denver Botanic Gardens' WaterSmart Garden and in zone 4b in Lauren's home garden.

Viola corsica

Corsican violet • Violaceae (violet family)

SIZE ▸ 6–8 in. tall and wide

FLOWERS ▸ violet-blue, spring through fall

BEST FEATURES ▸ vivid flowers; cold hardy; tolerates both sunny and shady exposures; long flowering season in cooler climates; spreads locally by self-seeding

Corsican violet is closely related to the pansy and shares many traits. It's prized for its hardiness and ability to flower in chilly weather. The bounty of pretty-faced, pansylike flowers throughout the year coupled with the ease of growing in a wide range of conditions gives gardeners everywhere reason to include Corsican violet.

CULTURE
Full sun to partial shade. Clay or loam. Moderate watering. Reseeds freely when established, but seedlings are easy to pull and can be transplanted to more suitable locations if desired. Propagate by seeds, which require a 30-day cold stratification before sowing. Also propagate with some success by stem cuttings. USDA hardiness zones 3–8.

LANDSCAPE USE
Corsican violet is useful as a low-growing groundcover around shrubs and under trees. It's a good companion plant in beds and borders with other perennials, annuals, ornamental grasses, or spring-flowering bulbs, and also works well in rock gardens. This lovely cool-weather plant mixes nicely with small groundcovers and perennials such as Turkish, CRYSTAL RIVER, and SNOWMASS blue-eyed veronicas; purple winter savory; and COLORADO GOLD gazania.

NATIVE RANGE AND ORIGIN
Corsica, Sardinia, and Elba islands (Italy), among spiny shrubs and in rocky meadows.

ORNAMENTAL GRASSES

Andropogon gerardii 'PWIN01S'

WINDWALKER **big bluestem** • Poaceae (grass family)

SIZE ▶ 6 ft. tall, 2 ft. wide

FLOWERS ▶ burgundy plumes, fall

BEST FEATURES ▶ tall, narrow, silvery blue foliage with deep red/burgundy fall color

In trials, plants maintained consistent habit exhibiting showy blue foliage all summer, turning deep red-purple in the fall. This is the first truly blue-foliaged big bluestem ornamental grass available for landscapes and gardens.

CULTURE

Full sun. Clay, loam, or sandy soil. Moderate watering to dry. Very low maintenance. Allow plant to stand through winter, then cut it back to the ground in spring. Provide adequate water to keep the plant growing and lush, especially during hot, dry spells. Propagate by division in early spring and summer. USDA hardiness zones 5–8.

LANDSCAPE USE

This tall, narrow, elegant selection of native grass is a wonderful substitute for nonnative and potentially invasive ornamental grasses. Use it as a focal point, for an interesting physical or visual barrier, with other large perennials, or mixed with a full complement of larger-scale landscape plants. Because of its height, it is an excellent choice for adding movement to designs as well. Be sure to combine it with other gregarious plants such as regal torchlily, Tennessee purple coneflower, chocolate flower, winecups, and Chieftain manzanita. Deer resistant.

NATIVE RANGE AND ORIGIN

Tall grass prairies and Great Plains of the United States. WIND-WALKER was selected from a row of seedling big bluestem by Bill Adams, Sunscapes Nursery in Pueblo, Colorado, for its unusual blue color as a young plant.

Calamagrostis brachytricha

Korean feather reed grass • Syn. *Calamagrostis arundinacea* • Poaceae (grass family)

SIZE ▶ 24–40 in. tall, 20–24 in. wide

FLOWERS ▶ burgundy-tinged plumes that mature to tan, late summer through fall

BEST FEATURES ▶ elegant clump-forming grass; long-lasting seed heads

This is a slow-spreading, late summer- to fall-blooming species of reed grass. It has large, dark pink-tinged flower plumes atop stems that rise above the foliage. The plumes mature to a light tan as the seeds ripen, but are not reliably persistent into winter. Foliage turns yellowish beige in fall. With feathery summer flowers and attractive fall and winter presence, this grass suits a variety of sites and conditions. Birds are attracted to the seeds.

CULTURE
Full sun to partial shade. Clay (including heavy clay which helps keep the roots moist), loam, and sandy soil. Moderate watering to dry. Because it may reseed readily, be sure to deadhead and remove unwanted seedlings. Cut it to the ground in early spring for a nice fresh look for the new season. Use a chunky wood mulch and grow on the dry side to discourage seedlings Propagate by seed or division. USDA hardiness zones 4–9.

LANDSCAPE USE
Korean feather reed grass can be used effectively as a mass planting, an accent, or in containers. It is late to bloom, but has large, showy plumes. Combine it with late-blooming perennials such as agastache, *Salvia greggii* selections, Denver Daisy black-eyed Susan, or tall stonecrop. In areas of partial shade, pair it with Cashmere sage, DENVER GOLD columbine, or Snow Angel coral bells. Attracts birds. Deer resistant.

NATIVE RANGE AND ORIGIN
Korea, moist woodlands of central and eastern Asia.

Melinis nerviglumis

PINK CRYSTALS ruby grass • Poaceae (grass family)

SIZE ▶ 20–24 in. tall, 12–15 in. wide

FLOWERS ▶ fluffy pink inflorescences, summer

BEST FEATURES ▶ showy inflorescences; bluish gray-green stems and leaves; densely tufted habit of growth; long-blooming

The blue-green clumps of leaves are attractive on their own; however, the shimmering pink and silver inflorescences that appear in late summer create a flowering spectacle that continues until hard frost. This annual grass needs to be replanted seasonally.

CULTURE

Full sun to partial shade. Loam. Moderate watering. Planting larger plants results in earlier bloom and a longer season of interest. Propagate by seeds; sow seeds indoor in midwinter to achieve larger plants at transplanting time. USDA hardiness zones 4–6 as an annual, perennial in warmer climates

LANDSCAPE USE

PINK CRYSTALS ruby grass is lovely as an accent plant, in mass plantings and drifts, in mixed perennial or annual borders, planters, containers, raised beds, or wildflower meadow gardens. It can be combined with the Mexicali penstemons, Tennessee purple coneflower, SPANISH PEAKS foxglove, and Cheyenne mock orange. Deer resistant.

NATIVE RANGE AND ORIGIN

Sub-Saharan Africa and Madagascar. During the 1980s PINK CRYSTALS ruby grass was grown at Denver Botanic Gardens from seeds distributed by the Drakensberg Botanic Garden in Harrismith, Republic of South Africa (now Harrismith Wildflower Gardens). For many years this annual grass added beautiful accent to many display gardens.

Muhlenbergia reverchonii 'PUND01S'

UNDAUNTED ruby muhly, UNDAUNTED seep muhly • Poaceae (grass family)

SIZE ▶ 16–20 in. tall (24–30 in. in bloom), 18–24 in. wide

FLOWERS ▶ rosy inflorescences, fall

BEST FEATURES ▶ stunning ruby clouds of tiny flowers in autumn; fine-textured gray-green mounds of slender foliage; seed heads turn rusty brown and remain attractive all winter; long-lived, with none of the dieback in the center that is so common among many species of ornamental bunch-grasses

UNDAUNTED ruby muhly is a medium-sized, long-lived native bunch-grass with beautiful reddish flowers similar to the beloved but less hardy, less drought-tolerant Gulf muhly (*Muhlenbergia capillaris*). It is also known as seep muhly for its native haunts in Texas that are often saturated in the spring only to dry out completely in the heat and drought of summer.

CULTURE

Full sun. Clay or loam. Moderate watering to dry. Cut back finished flower stalks and previous year's foliage in early spring to make way for new growth. Tolerates seasonal water-logging as well as drought. Plants grow most vigorously with regular water, and grow more slowly and bloom less profusely if planted in sandy soil or under drier conditions. Propagate by division during active growth (warm-season grass). Also propagate by seed, which needs no pretreatment. USDA hardiness zones 5–10.

LANDSCAPE USE

UNDAUNTED ruby muhly is superb in mass plantings, as well as for accents or erosion control. Plant it to catch low-angled morning or afternoon light for best effects. Combine it with curly leaf sea kale, agastaches, moon carrot, Sea Foam sage, regal torchlily, and *Salvia greggii* selections. Deer resistant.

NATIVE RANGE AND ORIGIN

Southern Great Plains, Texas Hill Country. UNDAUNTED ruby muhly is an extra-robust selection brought from the northern Texas plains by plantspeople Scott and Lauren Ogden, and first trialed in Colorado in their Fort Collins garden in 2003 where it still thrives. They shared divisions and seed with nurseryman David Salman who produced commercial numbers quickly and began offering it a few years later through his mail-order company High Country Gardens as Autumn Embers muhly.

Sporobolus wrightii

Giant sacaton • Poaceae (grass family)

SIZE ▸ 5–7 ft. tall, 4–5 ft. wide

FLOWERS ▸ golden inflorescences, late summer

BEST FEATURES ▸ statuesque, xeric grass; wispy appearance; yellow fall color; native; seeds provide food for birds, especially in winter

Recommended by Plant Select in 2006, this is a xeric, native grass from the Great Plains. Flowering stalks (culms), produced in late summer, can easily reach 6 feet in height. The sturdy panicles of flowers produce reddish brown seeds and ultimately become golden and wispy. The leaves turn a lovely golden color in fall, providing winter interest. Native Americans ground the seed for flour and bound the stems for brushes.

CULTURE

Full sun to partial shade. Clay, loam, or sandy soil. Moderate watering to xeric. Plant in a location away from sidewalks where it will have room to grow. As with all ornamental grasses, leave the seed heads for winter interest and bird forage. Cut plants back in spring to 6–12 in. above the ground, being careful not to cut new stalks, or culms. Propagate by seed, which germinates readily with no pretreatment, or by divisions.

LANDSCAPE USE

Giant sacaton is an excellent specimen plant. Tall and graceful, it can stand alone or make an imposing hedge or privacy barrier. It can be used in place of more moisture-loving, nonnative large ornamental grasses, such as maiden or pampas grass (*Miscanthus* spp.). Useful in erosion control, it makes good cover and forage for small animals. It is also suitable in the back of a border, on difficult slopes, or as a focal point in xeriscape gardens. Giant sacaton combines well with large-statured perennials such as VERMILION BLUFFS Mexican sage, Maximillian sunflowers (*Helianthus maximiliana*), and WINDWALKER big bluestem, as well as with southwestern native shrubs such as fernbush, baby blue rabbitbrush, and Apache plume. Deer resistant.

NATIVE RANGE AND ORIGIN

Southwestern United States into Mexico.

VINES

Dolichos lablab 'Ruby Moon'

Ruby Moon hyacinth bean • Fabaceae (bean family)

SIZE ▶ 6-10 ft. trellised, 3–5 ft. untrellised

FLOWERS ▶ violet-purple, all summer

BEST FEATURES ▶ purple-hued foliage; rapidly growing vine; long season of appeal; provides a seasonal screen

Ruby Moon hyacinth bean is a vigorous vining cousin to garden beans but with dark purple tinged foliage, attractive in its own right. The generous clusters of deep amethyst-violet flowers resemble those of a delicate wisteria and are produced abundantly from midsummer to the frosty days of autumn.

CULTURE
Full sun to partial shade. Loam. Moderate watering. Susceptible to spider mites. Propagate by seed; collect seeds in the fall to sow in the greenhouse the following spring so that sizeable plants can be transplanted into the garden after frost-free date; soak them in hot water for an hour to help improve germination. USDA hardiness zones 7–11.

LANDSCAPE USE
Ruby Moon hyacinth bean makes a wonderful addition to a wall, fence, arbor, or pergola, creating graceful mounds in the annual or perennial border. By late summer, expect this plant to be a focal point in your garden with hundreds of flowers produced together with huge, flat, dark violet glossy legumes contrasting with purple leaves. Complement Ruby Moon's flower and bean colors with PIKE'S PEAK PURPLE, Carolyn's Hope, and SHADOW MOUNTAIN penstemons, and use silver-heels horehound to accent the lovely hues of purples and pinks. Attracts bees.

NATIVE RANGE AND ORIGIN
Tropical Africa and widely cultivated in India, Southeast Asia, Eqypt, and Sudan.

Arctostaphylos ×coloradoensis

Mock bearberry manzanita • Ericaceae (heath family)

SIZE ▶ 10–24 in. tall, 3–5 ft. wide

FLOWERS ▶ small bell-shaped, white deepening to pink, late winter to early spring

BEST FEATURES ▶ evergreen groundcover that is both sun- and drought-tolerant; early season flowers for bees.

Mock bearberry is the lowest-growing of the three manzanita selections introduced by Plant Select. It is a dense, prostrate form with smooth cinnamon-red to purplish exfoliating bark and bright green elliptical evergreen leaves. This selection performs much better than the others in heavier soil, but is best grown in sandy loam. Red fruits are sometimes produced in early fall.

CULTURE

Full sun to partial shade. Loam or sandy, well-drained soil. Moderate watering to xeric. In winters with little or no snow cover, provide supplemental water. Remove occasional dead branches in spring. Propagate by cuttings. USDA hardiness zones 4b–8.

LANDSCAPE USE

Use mock bearberry as an evergreen groundcover or low-growing shrub for informal mass plantings in sun or dappled shade. It can be planted with a variety of plants with similar needs, acting as a foil for other more colorful or structurally interesting forms. Attracts bees. Deer resistant.

NATIVE RANGE AND ORIGIN

Thought to be hybrids of *Arctostaphylos uva-ursi* (kinnickinnick) and *A. patula*, a shrubby form of manzanita; both western Colorado natives. Selected for its form and propagation qualities and brought to Plant Select by Betsy Baldwin-Owens.

Arctostaphylos ×*coloradoensis* 'Chieftain'

Chieftain manzanita • Ericaceae (heath family)

SIZE ▸ 1–3 ft. tall, 5–6 ft. wide

FLOWERS ▸ small bell-shaped, bright pink fading to white, late winter through early spring

BEST FEATURES ▸ broadleaved evergreen with beautiful mahogany-colored stems and bark; xeric once established

Chieftain is taller and more open-growing than the other manzanita selections introduced by Plant Select. As it matures it becomes a somewhat spreading and mounding shrub with beautiful year-round interest. The smooth cinnamon-red to purplish exfoliating bark is accentuated by the bright green oval leaves. Flowers appear in late winter and are often the first flowers to provide food for bees. Red fruits are sometimes produced in early fall.

CULTURE
Full sun to partial shade. Loam or sandy, well-drained soil. Moderate watering to xeric. Remove occasional dead branches in spring. Provide supplemental water during dry winter months if needed. Propagate by cuttings. USDA hardiness zones 5–8.

LANDSCAPE USE
Colorado manzanitas make an excellent evergreen mass, planted as a transition between a shrub bed and a lawn. Useful planted in a semishady site under trees and among rocks. They also look good in a rock garden or xeriscape. Plant Chieftain in combination with other western natives such as Grand Mesa penstemon, Blonde Ambition blue grama grass, and dwarf or Blue Jazz piñon pines. Attracts bees. Deer resistant.

NATIVE RANGE AND ORIGIN
Chieftain is a selection of a natural hybrid, *Arctostaphylos* ×*coloradoensis*, most likely between *A. uva-ursi*, a low-growing groundcover, and *A. patula*, found in western Colorado. It was brought to Plant Select by Betsy Baldwin-Owens.

Buddleja alternifolia 'Argentea'

Silver fountain butterfly bush • Loganiaceae (logania family)

SIZE ▶ 12–15 ft. tall, 10–12 ft. wide

FLOWERS ▶ lavender-blue, late spring

BEST FEATURES ▶ attractive bright lavender-blue flowers and silvery leaves; corky bark that shreds with age; thrives in a variety of sites and soil

---

The genus name honors Rev. Adam Buddle (1660–1715), English botanist and vicar of Farmbridge in Essex. The cultivar 'Argentea' has attractive leaves that are more silvery than the original *Buddleja alternifolia* and has proven to be at least one USDA plant hardiness zone hardier. It is also smaller and more shrublike than the species. In fact, it is the only butterfly bush that is reliably shrubby in much of the continental United States. The long slender stems give the plant a soft spreading and pendulous mounding habit. The fragrant flowers are tubular, lavender-blue to violet-purple with an orange throat, and appear early in the growing season.

CULTURE

Full sun to partial shade. Clay, loam, or sandy soil. Moderate watering; tolerates moist conditions. Flowers are produced only on old wood, so heavy pruning in the spring may eliminate next year's flowers. Following blooming, the flowering stems (12–30 in.) dry and die back. This makes the plant somewhat unattractive for 3–4 weeks until the new, silvery growth fills in and covers up the dried flower stems. The dried stalks can be pruned out but that will be quite time consuming on older plants. With time, a plant can also be pruned to form a small, multistemmed tree if desired. Propagate by hardwood cuttings taken from late spring through early summer. Also propagate by layering, but be sure to relocate rooted layers before plants break dormancy in spring. USDA hardiness zones 4–8.

LANDSCAPE USE

Silver fountain butterfly bush integrates well in shrub borders and also is suitable as a specimen in a mixed border or lawn setting or an informal hedge. Combine it with large-statured perennials such as WINDWALKER big bluestem or WINDWALKER royal red salvia, or with flowering shrubs including Ruby Voodoo rose and Carol Mackie daphne. Attracts butterflies and moths. Deer resistant.

NATIVE RANGE AND ORIGIN

The species is native to dry slopes in central and east-central China. The cultivar is named *argentea*, meaning "silver," in reference to the appearance produced by tiny hairs on the foliage. This attractive selection was introduced by Hillier Nursery in England in 1939.

Cercocarpus intricatus

Littleleaf mountain mahogany • Rosaceae (rose family)

SIZE ▶ 4–5 ft. tall, 3–4 ft. wide

FLOWERS ▶ Inconspicuous, yellow-green, summer

BEST FEATURES ▶ dark green foliage year-round; compact form; extreme drought tolerance

Few shrubs can tolerate the extreme heat, drought, and abuse that littleleaf mountain mahogany thrives on in its native habitat. It forms dense mounds on sheer cliffs subjected to weeks of 100°F+ heat in summer and subzero cold for weeks in the winter. Few plants can make a more uniform and satisfying dense hedge, screen or specimen in a sunny garden.

CULTURE
Full sun. Clay, loam, or sandy soil. Moderate watering to xeric. Establishes quickly and easily when started from a gallon or larger container. Water deeply every few weeks in dry weather, and after a year it will be virtually maintenance-free. Best planted in a hot, well-drained exposure where it is not watered excessively. Tends to grow more open in rich soil or moister conditions. Propagate by seed sown in winter. USDA hardiness zones 3–9.

LANDSCAPE USE
Littleleaf mountain mahogany responds extremely well to tip pruning and so is a great native plant option for formal hedging or topiary. It makes an excellent year-round feature for a xeric rock garden and would likely make a superb subject for a native bonsai since it develops a heavy trunk rather quickly and responds to shaping. It can be used as a backdrop to other native plant selections, including ORANGE CARPET hummingbird trumpet, red birds in a tree, and Blonde Ambition blue grama and Standing Ovation little bluestem grasses. Attracts inconspicuous small flies and bees, but is not important for honey production. Deer resistant.

NATIVE RANGE AND ORIGIN
Wyoming south to New Mexico and west to California.

Chamaebatiaria millefolium

Fernbush • Rosaceae (rose family)

SIZE ▸ 3–5 ft. tall and wide

FLOWERS ▸ white, in summer

BEST FEATURES ▸ white panicles of flowers for most of the summer; cinnamon-colored stems; aromatic foliage; xeric

Fernbush is a superb species for attracting bees to the garden. The plant has an interesting fragrance from the oils produced by the leaves and was used by indigenous tribes to make a tea. The fernlike leaves remain, though in a less prominent state, through winter, offering a bit of interest during the off season.

CULTURE

Full sun to partial shade. Clay, loam, or sandy soil. Moderate watering to xeric. To grow as a specimen plant, prune yearly to keep the plant healthy and get rid of any branches that are growing too vigorously. To grow as a sheared hedge, cut and shape plants once in the spring and again in mid- to late summer. Propagate by seeds, which need a 14- to 30-day cold stratification; do not cover as seeds need light to germinate. USDA hardiness zones 4b–8.

LANDSCAPE USE

This showy shrub can be used either as a specimen planting or maintained as a shrub in a mass planting. Plants tolerate shearing and can be shaped into more tidy shrubs and used in hedges. Fernbush can be planted with larger perennials such as VERMILION BLUFFS Mexican sage and desert penstemon, underplanted with ice plants, mixed with large grasses such as giant sacaton, or combined with other xeric shrubs including Apache plume, littleleaf mountain mahogany, and bluestem joint fir. Attracts bees. Deer resistant.

NATIVE RANGE AND ORIGIN

Lower to middle elevations in the Sierra Nevada range; most common on the eastern slope; can be found throughout the Great Basin.

Cytisus purgans

SPANISH GOLD broom • Fabaceae (bean family)

SIZE ▶ 3–4 ft. tall, 5–6 ft. wide

FLOWERS ▶ yellow, mid- to late spring

BEST FEATURES ▶ twiggy yet neat mound of evergreen stems; profusion of fragrant rich yellow pea flowers; stems remain green all winter when not wind-desiccated

There is always need for hardier, xeric, flowering shrubs, as shrubs are ideal plants for small spaces and very low maintenance. *Cytisus purgans* is one such plant. A gorgeous massive specimen of SPANISH GOLD broom was planted in 1983 by Panayoti Kelaidis in the Rock Alpine Garden at Denver Botanic Gardens and thrived there for many years. Placed in a prominent raised position toward the front and center of that garden, the plant drew much attention for its spectacular bloom and interesting form and texture, landing the species a spot with Plant Select.

CULTURE

Full sun to partial shade. Well-drained clay, loam, or sandy soil. Moderate watering to dry. Protect plant from strong winter winds that will desiccate it, turning stems brown and damaging flower buds. For a compact, dense plant, cut it back immediately after flowering so as not to lose any of next spring's flowers since buds are set on the previous season's growth. Plants grown in well-drained soil are longer-lived and more floriferous. Propagate by early summer cuttings or by scarified seed. USDA hardiness zones 4a–9.

LANDSCAPE USE

SPANISH GOLD broom provides early color in the sunny shrub border, and its good form and winter interest make it valuable as a focal point or a foundation plant. Its dense structure offers wildlife shelter and nesting habitat. This broom is more cold hardy and more tolerant of heavy soil than Scottish broom (*C. scoparius*) hybrids and selections and it is not invasive as are the hybrid Scottish brooms in some areas. Combine SPANISH GOLD broom with curly leaf sea kale, groundcovering veronicas, silver sage, Colorado desert blue star, Colorado manzanitas, or PLATINUM sage. Attracts bees. Deer resistant.

NATIVE RANGE AND ORIGIN

Mountains of France and Spain, into Portugal and Morocco.

Daphne ×*burkwoodii* 'Carol Mackie'

Carol Mackie daphne • Thymeleaceae (daphne family)

SIZE ▸ 3–4 ft. tall and wide

FLOWERS ▸ pink, spring

BEST FEATURES ▸ intensely fragrant clusters of flowers in spring and sporadically later; compact form; small, variegated leaves

At the time Carol Mackie daphne was promoted by Plant Select in 1997, daphnes were rarely utilized as landscape plants in much of the United States. Having proven itself for many years at Denver Botanic Gardens, this semievergreen, compact shrub with intensely fragrant flowers and variegated foliage was an irresistible choice for Plant Select to promote in its inaugural year. Once an obscure cultivar from New Jersey, Carol Mackie daphne was named for the gardener who discovered this showy specimen in her garden, and it has become the most widely planted daphne across America—and other daphnes are following in its wake.

CULTURE
Full sun to partial shade. Loam. Moderate watering to dry. Generally carefree in the garden, requiring minimal irrigation once established. Responds very well to pruning. Shape it gently—light shearing will keep the plant in bounds, yet growing vigorously. Plants kept compact with pruning are less susceptible to snow load damage. Propagate by cuttings under greenhouse conditions; easiest of all daphnes to root. USDA hardiness zones 4a–9.

LANDSCAPE USE
Carol Mackie daphne is best as a specimen in a border or shrub planting. It responds well to shearing, so it can make an excellent informal hedge. It's often used along foundations, where it grows well due to the protected habitat and the added lime from the neighboring building. Medium- to large-statured perennials such as curly leaf sea kale and Tennessee purple coneflower play off the foliage nicely, as do Colorado manzanitas and ground-covering veronicas. Attracts bees, butterflies, and moths.

NATIVE RANGE AND ORIGIN
A hybrid between Eurasian species *Daphne caucasica* (Caucasus) and *D. cneorum* (Spain to southwestern Russia).

Fallugia paradoxa

Apache plume • Rosaceae (rose family)

SIZE ▶ 4–6 ft. tall and wide

FLOWERS ▶ pale pink to white, summer

BEST FEATURES ▶ pale pink to white single flowers and attractive, wispy, dark pink seed heads from spring until frost; xeric once established; birds are attracted to seeds

Recommended by Plant Select in 2002, this underused southwestern native shrub gets its specific name *paradoxa* from its characteristic of being covered with both flowers and seeds simultaneously. These features create a highly dramatic display from spring to frost, forming a seemingly pink veil over the large shrub. Its finely textured foliage resists hail damage and provides an airy winter appearance, making it a four-season shrub. Native Americans used parts of this plant for ceremonial and medicinal purposes.

CULTURE

Full sun to partial shade. Clay, loam, or sandy soil. Moderate watering to xeric; dislikes wet conditions. Plant away from sidewalks where it has room to grow. If needed, it can be cut back severely (even to 1 ft.) to refresh it. Propagate by fresh seed, which germinates quickly; older seeds can have dormancies that are difficult to overcome. Also propagate by layering or removal of suckers. USDA hardiness zones 4–8.

LANDSCAPE USE

Apache plume is useful for wildlife cover and forage and erosion control. It is attractive as an accent plant backlit by the sun, in hedges, or in native designs. It is stunning when planted near purple-leaved plants to play off the color of the seed heads, or in mixed plantings with other western native plants including fernbush, littleleaf mountain mahogany, and Colorado manzanitas. Attracts bees, moths, hummingbirds, and butterflies. Deer resistant.

NATIVE RANGE AND ORIGIN

California to Colorado, south to Oklahoma, Texas, and north-central Mexico.

Jamesia americana

Waxflower • Hydrangeaceae (hydrangea family)

SIZE ▶ 4–6 ft. tall and wide

FLOWERS ▶ white, spring

BEST FEATURES ▶ tolerates dry shade; attractive reddish brown peeling bark; fragrant flowers; bright green foliage that changes to pinkish-orange shades in fall

This beautiful native shrub deserves a greater presence in western gardens. Waxflower refers to the fragrant, waxy, white flowers that appear in late spring and early summer over small, heavily textured green leaves that extend interest in the fall when they transform with autumnal hues. In addition to its natural beauty, waxflower is quite drought tolerant and is especially suited for drier shaded areas. *Jamesia* acknowledges Edwin James, botanist for the Long Expedition, which surveyed the Front Range in 1820.

CULTURE

Full sun to partial shade. Well-drained loam. Moderate watering to dry. Needs little maintenance other than occasional light pruning for shape. Plants are slow-growing. Propagate seeds, which easily germinate when fresh; seed viability diminishes rapidly with age. USDA hardiness zones 3–8.

LANDSCAPE USE

Waxflower is a useful shrub as a specimen, accent, or background grouping in a border, foundation, or naturalistic landscape. The interesting bark is an attractive winter feature. Waxflower pairs especially well with Plant Select agastaches, Denver Daisy black-eyed Susan, SILVER BLADE evening primrose, CORAL CANYON twinspur, and SPANISH GOLD broom. Attracts bees and butterflies. Deer resistant.

NATIVE RANGE AND ORIGIN

Wyoming, Utah, New Mexico, Arizona, and into the Sierra Nevada of California.

Lonicera korolkowii 'Floribunda'

BLUE VELVET honeysuckle • Caprifoliaceae (honeysuckle family)

SIZE ▸ 10–12 ft. tall, 8–10 ft. wide

FLOWERS ▸ pink, early spring

BEST FEATURES ▸ vase-shaped growth habit; bluish green foliage; tolerates a wide range of soil types and sites; resistant to honeysuckle witches' broom aphids

The attractive silvery blue foliage and floriferous nature (hence 'Floribunda') sets this honeysuckle apart from the more common Tatarian honeysuckle (*Lonicera tatarica*). Opalescent pink flowers are showy in early spring. 'Floribunda' is resistant to honeysuckle witches' broom aphids and the disfiguring growths that result from infestations. The species name commemorates General N. J. Korolikov, a Russian botanist who collected plants in central Asia in the 1870s.

CULTURE
Full sun to partial shade. Clay, loam, or sandy soil. Moderate watering to xeric. Avoid planting it too close to walks. Prune out any dead wood in spring after the new growth has started to emerge. Even as a very old plant this mounding honeysuckle retains its foliage to the ground if given enough room, unlike many other shrub honeysuckles. Propagate by semihardwood cuttings taken from late spring through early summer; insert cuttings in sand or containers with a well-draining medium. USDA hardiness zones 3–8.

LANDSCAPE USE
Use BLUE VELVET honeysuckle as a specimen, as a background plant in a large mixed border, or for massing in large areas. This large shrub is best paired with large-statured perennials such as WINDWALKER big bluestem and curly leaf sea kale, or in a mixed shrub border with MINI MAN or Alleghany viburnum. Attracts hawk moths. Deer resistant.

NATIVE RANGE AND ORIGIN
Hindu Kush mountain range of northern Afghanistan and Pakistan and the southern Tian Shan of Kazakhstan. The original plants of this variety were sent to the USDA Cheyenne Horticultural Field Station by Sutherland Nursery of Boulder, Colorado. This clone was selected from mature plants that had persisted for decades at the Cheyenne Station, noted for its harsh climate.

Philadelphus lewisii 'PWY01S'

CHEYENNE mock orange • Hydrangeaceae (hydrangea family)

SIZE ▶ 6–7 ft. tall, 8–10 ft. wide

FLOWERS ▶ white, spring through midsummer

BEST FEATURES ▶ fragrant, large white flowers; attractive cinnamon-colored bark

CHEYENNE is more cold-hardy than *Philadelphus coronarius* varieties and consistently blooms with a greater profusion of blossoms. The stems of CHEYENNE form a billowy, pleasing mound covered with dark blue-green foliage. It becomes somewhat oval shaped with age. The four-petaled flower matures to 2 in. across, white with prominent yellow stamens with the fragrance of citrus from late spring to midsummer. The bark matures to a shiny cinnamon, the fruit is a capsule with many seeds, and the leaves are dark blue-green, deciduous, and covered with short, soft hairs. The species' name commemorates Meriwether Lewis (Lewis & Clark Expedition), who first collected it on their return trip through Idaho and Montana in 1806. The mock orange is the state flower of Idaho.

CULTURE

Full sun to partial shade. Dry clay or sandy loam. Moderate watering to dry. Prune periodically to encourage new stems. The plant is very sensitive to herbicide. Propagate only from softwood or semihardwood cuttings; intermittent mist is needed to keep cuttings from wilting. USDA hardiness zones 3–9.

LANDSCAPE USE

CHEYENNE mock orange is ideal for naturalistic landscapes, mixed shrub plantings, the background of a perennial border, or foundation plantings. Site it for early access to fragrant flowers. In mixed shrub borders, use it with Ruby Voodoo rose, Carol Mackie daphne, and viburnums for fragrant, multiseason, low-care interest. Attracts bees. Deer resistant.

NATIVE RANGE AND ORIGIN

Northwestern North America from Cascade Mountains eastward to Montana and Utah, south to California. This clone was selected at the USDA Cheyenne Horticultural Field Station where it survived decades of harsh Great Plains winters without supplemental water or care.

Rhus trilobata 'Autumn Amber'

Autumn Amber sumac • Anacardiaceae (sumac family)

SIZE ▶ 10–14 in. tall, 6–8 ft.+ wide

FLOWERS ▶ inconspicuous, yellow, late spring through early summer

BEST FEATURES ▶ ground-covering habit; glossy leaves; very xeric; fall amber color depending on seasonal conditions

Creeping Autumn Amber sumac is quickly becoming the go-to choice as a xeric deciduous groundcover option instead of wood mulch. It thrives under natural precipitation once established and is a beautiful and perfect plant for tough, open areas. The glossy green leaves of summer turn yellow in autumn.

CULTURE

Full sun. Soil: loam or sandy soil. Moderate watering to xeric. Minimal maintenance unless trying to shape the plant into a small space, in which case trim it once or twice a year. Use hand trimmers to prune horizontal branches that lay too close to the ground to use electric trimmers. The branches will eventually root down so if containment is desired it's best to keep branches trimmed on a regular basis. Fall leaf litter clean-up is generally not needed in windier locations, otherwise rake or blow the leaves in fall to remove leaf litter and debris. Propagate by cuttings, which are difficult to root. USDA hardiness zones 4–8.

LANDSCAPE USE

Use Autumn Amber sumac as an individual or in masses cascading over boulders or the edges of retaining walls. It does well in hot, sunny slopes and green roof situations, or can be used as a living mulch among tall shrubs. It can be planted under xeric shrubs such as fernbush, mixed in with bluestem joint fir or with other ground-covering shrubs such as PAWNEE BUTTES sand cherry and the Colorado manzanitas. Deer resistant.

NATIVE RANGE AND ORIGIN

The species is native to the western United States from Mexico to Canada and the cultivar was discovered in Littlefield, Texas (near Lubbock), growing out of limestone outcroppings.

Ribes uva-crispa Comanche

Comanche gooseberry • Grossulariaceae (currant family)

SIZE ▶ 2–3 ft. tall, 4–5 ft. wide

FLOWERS ▶ inconspicuous, white, summer

BEST FEATURES ▶ abundant sweet and juicy red berries in mid- to late summer

Comanche gooseberry is widely cultivated for its delicious fruits, which are used in desserts, for preserves, and for wine making. The red nickel-size berries are produced in such abundance that the weight of the fruit causes the branches of this short shrub to become nearly prostrate. Unfortunately, the edible berries are borne on stems armed with stout 2-in.-long thorns—in triplets at the nodes—so you want to pay attention when harvesting.

CULTURE

Full sun (with adequate water) to partial shade. Clay, loam, or sandy soil. Moderate watering. Begins bearing fruit on 2-year-old wood. Production decreases after the branch is 4 years old so remove all branches 4 years or older by pruning them to the ground. This allows the younger fruiting branches more sun and air circulation and promotes the health of the shrub. Be aware that the thorns curve back towards the crown so take extra precautions when pruning. Watch out for green currant sawfly worms during the summer; they will quickly defoliate the entire shrub if not controlled. They can be removed by hand or killed with insecticidal soap, pyrethrum, or neem oil sprays. Propagate by softwood cuttings taken in summer and rooted under intermittent mist. USDA hardiness zones 3–9.

LANDSCAPE USE

Comanche gooseberry is one of the best small fruits for a semisunny spot in the garden. It can be planted in rows 4 ft. apart for a market garden. For a fun kitchen-themed garden, plant it with Saint Theresa Seedless grape, rhubarb, and other small fruits such as strawberries. Attracts bees. Deer resistant.

NATIVE RANGE AND ORIGIN

The species is native to Great Britain south and east to the Caucasus Mountains of southwestern Asia, but this gooseberry was once known as Red Jacket and was grown in England 160 years ago. Imported into the United States in the 1930s, it proved to be a superior clone in a large gooseberry evaluation at the USDA Cheyenne Horticultural Station. During the 1950s the gooseberry trial was repeated and Red Jacket was still the champion due to its hardiness, productivity, and relative freedom from powdery mildew. In the interim, however, another gooseberry from Canada was also named 'Red Jacket'. Plant Select decided to rename it Comanche to avoid confusion with its Canadian cousin.

Rosa glauca

Redleaf rose • Syn. *Rosa rubrifolia* • Rosaceae (rose family)

SIZE ▸ 6–8 ft. tall, 6–10 ft. wide

FLOWERS ▸ pink, spring through summer

BEST FEATURES ▸ Deep purple foliage; purplish red stems; red-orange rose hips; yellow, copper, and red fall colors; single blossoms ranging from pastel pink to white; xeric

The elegantly simple flowers bloom all spring and into summer. The red-orange rose hips are highly desirable for their appearance, as are the beautiful mottled fall leaf colors of copper, reds, and yellows. When young, the plant appears to be more vase-shaped, but as it matures it grows into a beautifully arching shrub. In winter, the reddish-purple stems provide garden color. Though redleaf rose has been known in horticulture for more than 150 years, Plant Select felt its drought-tolerance and resilience to western garden conditions was underappreciated and should be promoted more within the region.

CULTURE

Full sun to partial shade. Clay, loam, or sandy soil. Moderate watering to xeric. Looks best and requires little to no maintenance when given enough space to grow. If dead canes appear over the years, prune occasionally. Do not deadhead so that showy hips will be produced, offering late fall through winter interest and wildlife benefits. Propagate by seed. USDA hardiness zones 3–9.

LANDSCAPE USE

Redleaf rose is a large arching shrub that best suits large borders where the single pink flowers can be enjoyed from a distance blooming against a backdrop of dark purplish foliage. This rose also adds unexpected color and texture to xeric landscapes. For a beautiful mixed border, combine it with Apache plume, bluestem joint fir, fernbush, WINDWALKER big bluestem, and giant sacaton. Attracts bees, butterflies, and moths. Deer resistant.

NATIVE RANGE AND ORIGIN

Mountains of southern Europe.

Rosa 'Ruby Voodoo'

Ruby Voodoo rose • Rosaceae (rose family)

SIZE ▶ 5–6 ft. tall, 4–5 ft. wide

FLOWERS ▶ pink, spring through summer

BEST FEATURES ▶ fragrant 3-in. double blossoms of fuchsia-pink beginning in early summer and lightly repeating throughout summer

Strong fragrance, large full flowers, vigorous growth habit, and great disease resistance—what more can a gardener ask of a rose? This exceptional selection has it all, and beautiful fuchsia-pink flowers to boot.

CULTURE
Full sun to partial shade. Clay, loam, or sandy soil. Moderate watering to dry. Because it is easy to root and grow on its own roots, it can be pruned moderately to keep it in bounds, without the worry that the rootstock will take over. Prune out any winter-injured wood in spring. Provide some winter watering to prevent desiccation in dry periods. Propagate by softwood cuttings taken in summer and rooted under intermittent mist. USDA hardiness zones 4–10.

LANDSCAPE USE
Ruby Voodoo rose can be planted as a specimen at the back of the border or in mass. Ideally it should be placed where it's easily accessible to enjoy the flowers' sweet scent. This rose works well in groupings with larger grasses such as giant sacaton grass, WINDWALKER big bluestem, and Standing Ovation little bluestem, or underplant it with shorter grasses such as UNDAUNTED ruby muhly or blue avena grass (*Helictotrichon sempervirens*). Attracts bees, butterflies, and moths; an excellent nectar source.

NATIVE RANGE AND ORIGIN
A garden cultivar bred in Denver in 1998 by rosarian John A. Starnes Jr. It was selected by staff at Fort Collins Wholesale Nursery because it showed both the least winter injury and no leaf diseases when overhead irrigated. The female parent is *Rosa* 'Général Jacqueminot, a French Hybrid Perpetual from 1853, and the male parent is *R.* 'Stephen's Big Purple', a hybrid tea rose bred in New Zealand in 1985.

Viburnum burejaeticum 'PO17S'

MINI MAN dwarf Manchurian viburnum • Adoxaceae (elderberry family)

SIZE ▶ 4–6 ft. tall and wide

FLOWERS ▶ white, spring

BEST FEATURES ▶ dwarf rounded shrub with clusters of white flowers in late spring; persistent red to blue-black fruit; xeric

Half the size of the other *Viburnum burejaeticum* seedlings, Mini Man exhibits a particularly beautiful dense, rounded growth habit. Most importantly, unlike many dwarf viburnum cultivars that are often lacking in a bountiful floral display, it is covered with attractive clusters of white flowers. It has proven itself to be moderately xeric and extremely cold-hardy, surviving -40°F on occasion in Montana.

CULTURE
Full sun to partial shade. Loam, but tolerates clay or sandy soil. Moderate watering to xeric. If needed, prune in early summer as the flower buds are formed the previous growing season. Dormant pruning, although effective, will prune off the flower clusters. Propagate by softwood tip cuttings 4–5 in. long, dipped in rooting compound and rooted under intermittent mist. USDA hardiness zones 3–7.

LANDSCAPE USE
MINI MAN is a wonderful choice as a foundation planting, especially under windows, as this dwarf shrub can easily be pruned if it begins to obscure the view as it gets older. It pairs well with larger perennials and grasses, as well as with other shrubs and small trees, including WINDWALKER royal red salvia, Carol Mackie daphne, and seven-son-flower. Attracts bees, flies, and moths. Deer resistant.

NATIVE RANGE AND ORIGIN
The species is native to northern China, Mongolia, and eastern Siberia. Clayton Berg and Scott Skogerboe discovered this dwarf selection of the species in a row of seedling Manchurian viburnums at Valley Nursery in Helena, Montana, in 1998.

Juniperus scopulorum 'Woodward'

Woodward columnar juniper • Cupressaceae (cypress family)

SIZE ▸ 20 ft. tall, 4 ft. wide

FLOWERS ▸ none

BEST FEATURES ▸ narrow, columnar growth habit; soft-textured, dark green foliage that turns gray-blue in winter

This selection of Rocky Mountain juniper is an elegant upright evergreen that stands up to the windiest conditions and sheds snow loads with grace. Although it is very columnar, it does not exhibit the typical multileader growth indicative of many columnar forms of juniper.

CULTURE
Full sun to partial shade. Clay, loam, or sandy soil. Moderate watering to xeric. Little to no pruning is needed to maintain the strongly columnar shape. Propagate by evergreen cuttings and grafting. USDA hardiness zones 3–9.

LANDSCAPE USE
This tall, narrow juniper makes a great living fence or accent plant in the landscape. Use its strong structural features to play off large grasses such as WINDWALKER big bluestem and giant sacaton, as well as redleaf rose and CHEYENNE mock orange. Attracts birds. Deer resistant.

NATIVE RANGE AND ORIGIN
The species is native to North America throughout the Rocky Mountains from Alberta to Texas and west to Oregon and Washington. Woodward was originally found by the Southern Great Plains Horticulture Station at Woodward, Oklahoma, growing in a planted windbreak. The staff propagated it and sent it to the Central Great Plains Horticulture Station at Cheyenne, Wyoming (later named the USDA Cheyenne Horticultural Field Station). The Woodward station destroyed all their plants, but plants still remain at the Cheyenne station.

Picea glauca 'Pendula'

Weeping white spruce ● Pinaceae (pine family)

SIZE ▶ 20–24 ft. tall, 4–6 ft. wide

FLOWERS ▶ none

BEST FEATURES ▶ upright, narrow form of white spruce with pendulous branches

This graceful conifer was chosen for its sculptural form, year-round beauty, easy care, and adaptability to a wide range of garden and landscape situations. For areas with regular winter snows, weeping white spruce is a particularly good choice because the draping branches easily shed snow loads. Growth rate is relatively rapid (1–2 feet per year) once the tree is established. This species also offers diversity to urban landscapes heavily planted with more traditional species of spruce and pine.

CULTURE
Full sun to partial shade. Loam or sandy soil. Moderate watering to dry. Stake the central branch (leader) upright to ensure straight growth. Water occasionally in winter in dry climates or when there's a lack of snow cover. Propagate by grafting, usually by conifer specialty nurseries only. USDA hardiness zones 3–8.

LANDSCAPE USE
This elegant conifer is an excellent evergreen choice for a landscape specimen or focal point. The tall narrow form has a small footprint and offers superb proportion near large homes with limited planting areas. In a large mixed planting, combine it with HOT WINGS Tatarian maple, MINI MAN dwarf Manchurian viburnum, Ruby Voodoo rose, and masses of Standing Ovation little bluestem and UNDAUNTED ruby muhly grasses for a stunning low-care landscape design.

NATIVE RANGE AND ORIGIN
The species is native to mountains of northern United States and Canada. The original plant of Pendula was selected from a native stand of white spruce near Guelph, Ontario.

Scientific name	Common/Trade name	Maximum height and width	Bloom season	
TENDER PERENNIALS AND ANNUALS				
Gazania krebsiana	TANAGER gazania	3 × 10 in.	sp–fall	
Plectranthus argentatus	silver dollar plant	36 × 40 in.	sum	
Rudbeckia 'Denver Daisy'	Denver Daisy black-eyed Susan	28 × 25 in.	sum–fall	
Scutellaria suffrutescens	cherry skullcap	8 × 15 in.	sp–fall	
PETITES				
Androsace sarmentosa 'Chumbyi'	silky rock jasmine	4 × 12 in.	sum	
Arenaria 'Wallowa Mountains'	Wallowa Mountains desert moss	½ × 12 in.	sp	
Clematis scottii	Scott's sugarbowls	12 × 15 in.	sp–sum	
Draba rigida	yellow stardust draba	3 × 10 in.	sp	
Geranium dalmaticum	Dalmatian pink cranesbill	8 × 8 in.	sp	
Heterotheca 'Goldhill'	Goldhill golden-aster	2 × 10 in.	sp–fall	
Heuchera pulchella	Sandia coral bells	10 × 8 in.	sp–sum	
Iris hookeri	dwarf beach-head iris	12 × 12 in.	sp	
Pinus edulis dwarf selections	dwarf piñon pine	30 × 30 in.	NA	
Pinus monophylla 'Blue Jazz'	Blue Jazz single-leaf piñon pine	30 × 30 in.	NA	
Primula elatior	oxlip primrose	12 × 15 in.	sp	
Pterocephalus depressus	Moroccan pincushion flower	3 × 12 in.	sp–sum	

Primary flower color	USDA hardiness zone	Exposure	Water needs	Wildlife	Special landscape use	North American roots
orange	6–9	full sun, partial shade	● ● ✕	bee		
white	10b–11	full sun, partial shade	● ●	bee		
yellow	6–9	full sun	● ●	bee, no deer		yes
red	6–9	full sun, partial shade	● ●	bee		yes
pink	3–8	partial shade, shade	● ✕	bee	dry shade, winter, cold hardy	
inconspicuous, white	4–8	full sun, partial shade	● ● ✕	bee, no deer	winter	yes
blue	4–7	full sun	● ● ✕	bee, no deer		yes
yellow	4–8	full sun, partial shade	● ● ✕	bee		
pink	5–8	full sun, partial shade	● ●	bee, no deer		
yellow	5–8	full sun	● ✕	bee, no deer		yes
pink	4–7	full sun, partial shade, shade	● ● ✕	bee, no deer	dry shade, winter	yes
blue	3–8	full sun, partial shade	● ●	bee, no deer		yes
NA	4–7	full sun	✕ ✕	no deer	winter	yes
NA	4–7	full sun	✕ ✕	no deer	winter	yes
yellow	4–8	partial shade, shade	● ●	bee, no deer	dry shade	
pink	4–8	full sun, partial shade	● ● ✕	bee, no deer		

Scientific name	Common/Trade name	Maximum height and width	Bloom season
GROUNDCOVERS			
Callirhoe involucrata	winecups	12 × 60 in.	sp–fall
Cynodon 'PWIN04S'	DOG TUFF grass	4 × 24 in.+	sum
Delosperma 'Alan's Apricot'	Alan's Apricot ice plant	2 × 18 in.	sp–sum
Delosperma dyeri 'Psdold'	RED MOUNTAIN ice plant	2 × 14 in.	sp–sum
Delosperma floribundum	STARBURST ice plant	4 × 12 in.	sum
Delosperma 'John Proffitt'	TABLE MOUNTAIN ice plant	2 × 20 in.	sum
Delosperma 'Kelaidis'	MESA VERDE ice plant	2 × 14 in.	sum
Delosperma 'P001S'	FIRE SPINNER ice plant	2 × 18 in.	sp–sum
Delosperma 'Psfave'	Lavender Ice ice plant	2 × 24 in.	sp–sum
Delosperma 'PWWG02S'	RED MOUNTAIN Flame ice plant	2 × 24 in.	sum
Eriogonum umbellatum var. *aureum* 'Psdowns'	KANNAH CREEK buckwheat	15 × 24 in.	sum
Marrubium rotundifolium	silverheels horehound	4 × 30 in.	sum
Paxistima canbyi	mountain lover	12 × 20 in.	sp
Sedum sediforme	Turquoise Tails blue sedum	10 × 18 in.	sum
Tanacetum densum subsp. *amani*	partridge feather	6 × 24 in.	sum
Verbena bipinnatifida	VALLEY LAVENDER plains verbena	6 × 18 in.	sp–fall
Veronica liwanensis	Turkish veronica	2 × 32 in.	sp
Veronica 'P018S'	SNOWMASS blue-eyed veronica	3 × 32 in.	sp

Primary flower color	USDA hardiness zone	Exposure	Water needs	Wildlife	Special landscape use	North American roots
magenta	3–9				dry shade	yes
inconspicuous	5–10					
apricot	4–9				winter	
red	5–8				winter	
purple	5–9				winter	
fuchsia	4–9				winter	
pink	4–8				winter	
multi	5–9				winter	
lavender	4–9				winter	
red	4–9				winter	
yellow	3–8				winter, cold hardy	yes
white	4–9				winter	
inconspicuous, green	4–9				winter	yes
yellow	5a–10				dry shade, winter	
yellow	4–9				winter	
purple	5–8					yes
blue	3–10				winter, cold hardy	
white	3–7				winter, cold hardy	

Scientific name	Common/Trade name	Maximum height and width	Bloom season	
GROUNDCOVERS (*cont.*)				
Veronica 'Reavis'	CRYSTAL RIVER veronica	3 × 32 in.	sp–sum	
Zinnia grandiflora 'Gold on Blue'	Gold on Blue prairie zinnia	10 × 18 in.	sum	
PERENNIALS				
Agastache aurantiaca 'P012S'	CORONADO hyssop	18 × 15 in.	sum–fall	
Agastache aurantiaca 'Pstessene'	CORONADO Red hyssop	18 × 15 in.	sum–fall	
Agastache cana 'Sinning'	SONORAN SUNSET hyssop	15 × 15 in.	sum–fall	
Agastache rupestris	sunset hyssop	24 × 20 in.	sum–fall	
Amsonia jonesii	Colorado desert blue star	15 × 15 in.	sp	
Anchusa capensis	summer forget-me-not	15 × 8 in.	sp–fall	
Anthemis marschalliana	filigree daisy	12 × 18 in.	sp	
Aquilegia chrysantha	DENVER GOLD columbine	36 × 20 in.	sp–sum	
Aquilegia 'Swan Violet & White'	REMEMBRANCE columbine	24 × 18 in.	sp–sum	
Artemisia versicolor 'Sea Foam'	Sea Foam sage	12 × 36 in.	sum	
Berlandiera lyrata	chocolate flower	20 × 20 in.	sum–fall	
Clematis integrifolia 'PSHarlan'	MONGOLIAN BELLS clematis	15 × 15 in.	sp–sum	
Crambe maritima	curly leaf sea kale	24 × 48 in.	sp–sum	
Dianthus	FIRST LOVE dianthus	20 × 15 in.	sp–fall	
Diascia integerrima 'P009S'	CORAL CANYON twinspur	18 × 15 in.	sum–fall	
Digitalis obscura	SUNSET foxglove	24 × 20 in.	sum	

Primary flower color	USDA hardiness zone	Exposure	Water needs	Wildlife	Special landscape use	North American roots
blue	3–7				winter, cold hardy	
yellow	4–8					yes
orange	5–9					yes
red	5–9					yes
pink	5–9					yes
light orange	4b–10					yes
blue	4–9					yes
blue	5–10					
yellow	4–10					
yellow	3–8				dry shade, cold hardy	yes
blue	3–9				cold hardy	yes
inconspicuous, greenish white	4b–8				winter	
yellow	4–9					yes
multi	3–9				cold hardy	
white	4–8					
pink	3b–9				cold hardy	
pink	4b–8					
orange	4b–9				winter	

Scientific name	Common/Trade name	Maximum height and width	Bloom season
PERENNIALS (*cont.*)			
Digitalis thapsi	SPANISH PEAKS foxglove	18 × 12 in.	sum
Echinacea tennesseensis	Tennessee purple coneflower	24 × 18 in.	sum
Echium amoenum	red feathers	16 × 8 in.	sp–sum
Engelmannia peristenia	Engelmann's daisy	28 × 18 in.	sum
Epilobium fleischeri	alpine willowherb	20 × 12 in.	sp–sum
Eriogonum wrightii var. *wrightii*	Snow Mesa buckwheat	20 × 24 in.	sum
Erodium chrysanthum	golden storksbill	10 × 24 in.	sp–sum
Gazania linearis 'P004S'	COLORADO GOLD gazania	6 × 12 in.	sp–fall
Geranium magniflorum 'P013S'	LA VETA LACE geranium	10 × 24 in.	sp–sum
Heuchera sanguinea 'Snow Angel'	Snow Angel coral bells	15 × 12 in.	sp–sum
Kniphofia caulescens	regal torchlily	40 × 30 in.	sum
Linum narbonense	Narbonne blue flax	18 × 18 in.	sp–sum
Monardella macrantha 'Marian Sampson'	hummingbird trumpet mint	6 × 12 in.	sp–sum
Nepeta 'Psfike'	LITTLE TRUDY catmint	15 × 15 in.	sp–fall
Oenothera macrocarpa subsp. *incana*	SILVER BLADE evening primrose	8 × 24 in.	sp–sum
Origanum libanoticum	hopflower oregano	15 × 24 in.	sum–fall
Osteospermum 'Avalanche'	Avalanche white sun daisy	14 × 24 in.+	sp–sum
Osteospermum barberiae var. *compactum* 'P005S'	PURPLE MOUNTAIN sun daisy	14 × 14 in.	sp–sum

Primary flower color	USDA hardiness zone	Exposure	Water needs	Wildlife	Special landscape use	North American roots
pink	4b–9	sun, part shade, shade	💧💧	bee, no deer	dry shade	
pink	5–7	sun, part shade	💧💧	bee, no deer		yes
red	3–9	sun, part shade	💧💧🗴	bee, no deer	cold hardy	
yellow	5–10	sun, part shade	💧💧🗴	bee, no deer		yes
pink	3–8	sun, part shade	💧	bee	cold hardy	
white	4–9	sun	🗴🗴	bee, no deer	winter	yes
yellow	4–9	sun, part shade	💧💧🗴	bee, no deer		
yellow	4a–8	sun, part shade	💧🗴🗴	bee		
purple	4–8	sun, part shade	💧💧	bee	winter	
red	3–9	part shade, shade	💧🗴	bee, no deer	dry shade, cold hardy	yes
orange	4b–9	sun, part shade	💧💧	bee, no deer		
blue	5–8	sun, part shade	💧💧🗴	bee, no deer	winter	
red	5b–9	part shade	💧🗴	bee, no deer	dry shade	yes
blue	4–9	sun, part shade	💧💧🗴	bee, no deer	cold hardy	
yellow	4a–9	sun	💧💧🗴	bee, no deer		yes
lavender	4–8	sun, part shade	💧🗴🗴	bee, no deer	winter	
white	4–9	sun, part shade	💧💧🗴	bee		
purple	4b–9	sun, part shade	💧💧	bee		

Scientific name	Common/Trade name	Maximum height and width	Bloom season	
PERENNIALS (*cont.*)				
Osteospermum 'P006S'	LAVENDER MIST sun daisy	14 × 16 in.	sp–sum	
Penstemon 'Coral Baby'	Coral Baby penstemon	15 × 15 in.	sp–sum	
Penstemon grandiflorus 'P010S'	PRAIRIE JEWEL penstemon	36 × 12 in.	sum	
Penstemon linarioides var. coloradoensis 'P014S'	SILVERTON bluemat penstemon	12 × 15 in.	sp–sum	
Penstemon mensarum	Grand Mesa penstemon	30 × 15 in.	sp	
Penstemon ×mexicali 'Carolyn's Hope'	Carolyn's Hope penstemon	18 × 14 in.	sum	
Penstemon ×mexicali 'P007S'	PIKE'S PEAK PURPLE penstemon	18 × 14 in.	sum	
Penstemon ×mexicali 'P008S'	RED ROCKS penstemon	18 × 14 in.	sum	
Penstemon ×mexicali 'Psmyers'	SHADOW MOUNTAIN penstemon	24 × 18 in.	sum	
Penstemon ×mexicali 'PWIN02S'	WINDWALKER Garnet penstemon	18 × 14 in.	sum	
Penstemon pseudospectabilis	desert penstemon	36 × 20 in.	sp–sum	
Penstemon rostriflorus	Bridges' penstemon	36 × 36 in.	sum	
Phlomis cashmeriana	cashmere sage	60 × 30 in.	sum	
Salvia argentea	silver sage	36 × 24 in.	sum	
Salvia daghestanica	PLATINUM sage	10 × 18 in.	sum	
Salvia darcyi 'Pscarl'	VERMILION BLUFFS Mexican sage	40 × 30 in.	sum–fall	
Salvia 'PWIN03S'	WINDWALKER royal red salvia	48 × 36 in.	sum–fall	
Salvia greggii 'Furman's Red'	Furman's Red autumn sage	24 × 24 in.	sum–fall	

Primary flower color	USDA hardiness zone	Exposure	Water needs	Wildlife	Special landscape use	North American roots
lavender	4b–8	sun, part shade	2 drops (1 crossed)	bee		
coral	5–8	sun	2 drops (1 crossed)	bee, no deer		yes
multi	3–9	sun	2 drops (crossed)	bee, no deer	cold hardy	yes
blue	4–10	sun, part shade	2 drops (crossed)	bee, no deer	winter	yes
blue	3–9	sun, part shade	3 drops (1 crossed)	bee, no deer	winter, cold hardy	yes
pink	4b–8	sun, part shade	2 drops	bee, no deer		yes
purple	4b–8	sun, part shade	2 drops	bee, no deer		yes
pink	4b–8	sun, part shade	2 drops	bee, no deer		yes
lavender	4b–8	sun, part shade	2 drops	bee, no deer		yes
garnet	4b–8	sun, part shade	2 drops	bee, no deer		yes
pink	5–9	sun, part shade	2 drops (crossed)	bee, no deer	winter	yes
red	4b–8	sun, part shade	3 drops (1 crossed)	bee, no deer	winter	yes
lavender	4b–8	sun, part shade	2 drops (1 crossed)	bee, no deer	dry shade, winter	
white	4a–10	sun, part shade	3 drops (1 crossed)	bee, no deer	winter	
blue	5–10	sun, part shade	2 drops (1 crossed)	bee, no deer	winter	
red	5b–10	sun, part shade	3 drops (1 crossed)	bee, no deer		yes
red	5–9	sun	3 drops (1 crossed)	bee, no deer		yes
red	5b–10	sun, part shade	3 drops (1 crossed)	bee, no deer		yes

Scientific name	Common/Trade name	Maximum height and width	Bloom season	
PERENNIALS (*cont.*)				
Salvia greggii 'Wild Thing'	Wild Thing autumn sage	24 × 24 in.	sum–fall	
Salvia pachyphylla	Mojave sage	24 × 30 in.	sum	
Salvia reptans 'P016S'	AUTUMN SAPPHIRE sage	24 × 24 in.	fall	
Satureja montana var. *illyrica*	purple winter savory	6 × 15 in.	sum–fall	
Scrophularia macrantha	red birds in a tree	36 × 20 in.	sum	
Scutellaria resinosa 'Smoky Hills'	Smoky Hills skullcap	10 × 14 in.	sum	
Seseli gummiferum	moon carrot	30 × 15 in.	sum–fall	
Tanacetum cinerariifolium	Dalmatian daisy	20 × 24 in.	sum	
Viola corsica	Corsican violet	8 × 8 in.	sp–fall	
Zauschneria garrettii 'PWWG01S'	ORANGE CARPET hummingbird trumpet	4 × 24 in.	sum	
ORNAMENTAL GRASSES				
Andropogon gerardii 'PWIN01S'	WINDWALKER big bluestem	6 × 2 ft.	fall	
Bouteloua gracilis 'Blonde Ambition'	Blonde Ambition blue grama grass	3 × 3 ft.	sum–fall	
Calamagrostis brachytricha	Korean feather reed grass	40 × 24 in.	sum–fall	
Melinis nerviglumis	PINK CRYSTALS ruby grass	24 × 15 in.	sum	
Muhlenbergia reverchonii 'PUND01S'	UNDAUNTED ruby muhly	30 × 24 in.	fall	
Schizachyrium scoparium 'Standing Ovation'	Standing Ovation little bluestem	36 × 18 in.	sum–fall	
Sporobolus wrightii	giant sacaton	7 × 5 ft.	sum	

Primary flower color	USDA hardiness zone	Exposure	Water needs	Wildlife	Special landscape use	North American roots
pink	5b–10	full sun, part shade	●●✕	bee, deer-resistant		yes
blue	5–10	full sun	✕●	bee, deer-resistant	winter	yes
blue	5–10	full sun, part shade	✕●	bee, deer-resistant		yes
purple	3b–8	full sun, part shade	●●✕	bee, deer-resistant	winter, cold hardy	
red	4–9	full sun, part shade	●●✕	bee		yes
blue	4–9	full sun	●✕	bee, deer-resistant		yes
white	5–9	full sun, part shade	●✕✕	bee, deer-resistant		
white	4–10	full sun, part shade	●●	deer-resistant		
purple	3–8	full sun, part shade	●		winter, cold hardy	
orange	3–8	full sun, part shade	●●✕	bee, deer-resistant	cold hardy	yes
burgundy	5–8	full sun	●✕	deer-resistant	winter	yes
chartreuse	4–9	full sun, part shade	●●✕	deer-resistant	winter, cold hardy	yes
burgundy	4–9	full sun, part shade	●✕	bee, deer-resistant	dry shade, winter	
pink	8–10	full sun, part shade	●	deer-resistant		
pink	5–10	full sun	●●	deer-resistant	winter	yes
pink	3–8	full sun	●●●	deer-resistant	winter, cold hardy	yes
gold	5–8	full sun, part shade	●✕	deer-resistant	winter	yes

Scientific name	Common/Trade name	Maximum height and width	Bloom season	
VINES				
Dolichos lablab 'Ruby Moon'	Ruby Moon hyacinth bean	10 × 5 ft.	sum	
Lonicera reticulata 'PO15S'	KINTZLEY'S GHOST honeysuckle	12 × 6 ft.	sum	
Vitis 'Saint Theresa Seedless'	Saint Theresa Seedless grape	20 × 8 ft.	sp	
SHRUBS				
Arctostaphylos ×coloradoensis	mock bearberry manzanita	24 × 60 in.	sp	
Arctostaphylos ×coloradoensis 'Chieftain'	Chieftain manzanita	3 × 6 ft.	sp	
Arctostaphylos ×coloradoensis 'Panchito'	Panchito manzanita	24 × 60 in.	sp	
Buddleja alternifolia 'Argentea'	silver fountain butterfly bush	15 × 12 ft.	sp	
Cercocarpus intricatus	littleleaf mountain mahogany	5 × 4 ft.	sum	
Chamaebatiaria millefolium	fernbush	5 × 5 ft.	sum	
Chrysothamnus nauseosus var. *nauseosus*	baby blue rabbitbrush	36 × 36 in.	sum	
Cytisus purgans	SPANISH GOLD broom	4 × 6 ft.	sp	
Daphne ×burkwoodii 'Carol Mackie'	Carol Mackie daphne	4 × 4 ft.	sp	
Ephedra equisetina	bluestem joint fir	5 × 8 ft.	sp	
Fallugia paradoxa	Apache plume	6 × 6 ft.	sum	
Hesperaloe parviflora	red yucca	4 × 2 ft.	sum–fall	
Jamesia americana	waxflower	6 × 6 ft.	sp	
Lonicera korolkowii 'Floribunda'	BLUE VELVET honeysuckle	12 × 10 ft.	sp	
Philadelphus lewisii 'PWY01S'	CHEYENNE mock orange	7 × 10 ft.	sp–sum	

Primary flower color	USDA hardiness zone	Exposure	Water needs	Wildlife	Special landscape use	North American roots
purple	7–11					
yellow	4–8					yes
inconspicuous, white	4–9					
pink	4b–8				dry shade winter	yes
pink	5–8				dry shade, winter	yes
pink	4b–8				dry shade, winter	yes
lavender	4–8					
inconspicuous, yellow	3–9				winter, cold hardy	yes
white	4b–8				winter	yes
yellow	4–9				winter	yes
yellow	4a–9				winter	
pink	4a–9				dry shade	
inconspicuous, yellow	4b–9				winter	
white	4–8					yes
red	5–10				winter	yes
white	3–8				dry shade, cold hardy	yes
pink	3–8				cold hardy	yes
white	3–9				cold hardy	yes

Scientific name	Common/Trade name	Maximum height and width	Bloom season	
SHRUBS (*cont.*)				
Prunus besseyi 'P011S'	PAWNEE BUTTES sand cherry	18 × 6 ft.	sp	
Rhus trilobata 'Autumn Amber'	Autumn Amber sumac	1 × 8 ft.+	sp–sum	
Ribes uva-crispa Comanche	Comanche gooseberry	3 × 5 ft.	sum	
Rosa glauca	redleaf rose	8 × 10 ft.	sp–sum	
Rosa 'Ruby Voodoo'	Ruby Voodoo rose	6 × 5 ft.	sp–sum	
Viburnum burejaeticum 'P017S'	MINI MAN dwarf Manchurian viburnum	6 × 6 ft.	sp	
Viburnum ×rhytidophylloides 'Alleghany'	Alleghany viburnum	10 × 10 ft.	sp	
TREES				
Acer tataricum 'GarAnn'	HOT WINGS Tatarian maple	18 × 18 ft.	sum	
Crataegus ambigua	Russian hawthorn	20 × 16 ft.	sp	
Heptacodium miconioides	seven-son-flower	25 × 15 ft.	sum	
Juniperus scopulorum 'Woodward'	Woodward columnar juniper	20 × 4 ft.	NA	
Picea glauca 'Pendula'	weeping white spruce	24 × 6 ft.	NA	

Primary flower color	USDA hardiness zone	Exposure	Water needs	Wildlife	Special landscape use	North American roots
white	3–8	sun, part shade	◐ drop, drop, ✕drop	bee	cold hardy	yes
inconspicuous, yellow	4–8	sun	drop, drop, ✕drop	no deer	winter	yes
inconspicuous, white	3–9	sun, part shade	drop	bee, no deer	cold hardy	
pink	3–9	sun, part shade	drop, drop, drop	bee, no deer	winter, cold hardy	
pink	4–10	sun, part shade	drop, drop	bee		
white	3–7	sun, part shade	drop, drop, ✕drop	bee, no deer	dry shade, cold hardy	
white	4b–8	sun, part shade, full shade	drop, drop	bee, no deer	dry shade, winter	
inconspicuous, green	4–10	sun, part shade	drop, ✕drop	bee		
white	4–9	sun, part shade	drop, ✕drop, ✕drop	bee, no deer	winter	
white	5–9	sun, part shade	drop, drop	bee	winter	
NA	3–9	sun, part shade	drop, drop, ✕drop	bee, no deer	winter, cold hardy	yes
NA	3–8	sun, part shade	drop, drop		winter, cold hardy	yes

FOR FURTHER READING

Bone, Michael, Dan Johnson, Panayoti Kelaidis, Mike Kintgen, and Larry G. Vickerman. 2015. *Steppes: The Plants and Ecology of the World's Semi-arid Regions.* Portland, Oregon: Timber Press.

Ellefson, Connie Lockhard, and David Winger. 2013. *Xeriscape Colorado: The Complete Guide.* Englewood, Colorado: Westliffe Publishers.

Kelaidis, Panayoti. 2009. *Flourish: A Visionary Garden in the American West.* Boulder, Colorado: 3D Press.

Knopf, Jim. 2005. *WaterWise Landscaping with Trees, Shrubs, and Vines: A Xeriscape Guide for the Rocky Mountain Region, California, and Desert Southwest.* 2nd edition. Boulder, Colorado: Chamisa Books.

Lehndorff, Betsy, and Laura Peters. 2007. *Best Garden Plants for Colorado.* Edmonton, Alberta, Canada: Lone Pine Publishing.

Meyer, Susan E., Roger K. Kjelgren, Darrel. G. Morrison, and William R. Varga. 2009. *Landscaping on the New Frontier: Waterwise Design for the Intermountain West.* Logan, Utah: Utah State University Press.

Nold, Robert. 1999. *Penstemons.* Portland, Oregon: Timber Press.

Nold, Robert. 2008. *High and Dry: Gardening with Cold-Hardy Dryland Plants.* Portland, Oregon: Timber Press.

Ogden, Lauren Springer. 2011. *The Undaunted Garden: Planting for Weather-Resilient Beauty.* 2nd edition. Golden, Colorado: Fulcrum Publishing.

Ogden, Scott, and Lauren Springer Ogden. 2008. *Plant-Driven Design: Creating Gardens That Honor Plants, Place, and Spirit.* Portland, Oregon: Timber Press.

Ogden, Scott, and Lauren Springer Ogden. 2011. *Waterwise Plants for Sustainable Gardens: 200 Drought-Tolerant Choices for All Climates.* Portland, Oregon: Timber Press.

Phillips, Judith. 1995. *Plants for Natural Gardens.* Albuquerque, New Mexico: Museum of New Mexico Press.

Phillips, Judith. 2015. *Growing the Southwest Garden.* Portland, Oregon: Timber Press.

Plant Select. 2009. *Durable Plants for the Garden.* Golden Colorado: Fulcrum Publishing.

Proctor, Rob, and Denver Water. 1996. *Xeriscape Plant Guide: 100 Water-wise Plants for Gardens and Landscapes.* Golden Colorado: Fulcrum Publishing.

Shaub, Sarah, and James Klett. 2014. *Dependable Landscape Trees.* Fort Collins, Colorado: Colorado State University Arboretum.

Tannehill, Celia, and James E. Klett. 2003. *Best Perennials for the Rocky Mounts and High Plains.* Rev. edition. Fort Collins, Colorado: Colorado State University Cooperative Extension.

Tatroe, Marcia. 2007. *Cutting Edge Gardening in the Intermountain West.* Boulder, Colorado: Johnson Books.

Weinstein, Gayle. 1999. *Xeriscape Handbook: A How-to Guide to Natural Resource-Wise Gardening.* Golden Colorado: Fulcrum Publishing.

ACKNOWLEDGMENTS

Both this book and the organization Plant Select are works of dedication and passion by many people with abundant talents. Many thanks go out to the people tasked with making this book come together: Sonya Anderson, Michael Bone, Pat Hayward, Panayoti Kelaidis, Jim Klett, Harriett McMillan, and David Winger. The nuances and details of editing were undertaken by Pat Hayward, Ann Frazier, Carla Tews, and Ronda Koski.

Plant profiles were written and reviewed by experts in the field: Ann Hartman-Mahr, Brian Core, Carolyn Toole, David Salman, Diana Reavis, Dianne Skogerboe, Gary Epstein, Gay Bechir, Ginger Jennings, Harriett McMillan, Jim Klett, Keith Williamson, Kirk Fieseler, Lauren Springer Ogden, Michael Bone, Mike Kintgen, Panayoti Kelaidis, Pat Hayward, Ross Shrigley, Scott Skogerboe, and Sonya Anderson.

A team of talented photographers provided the gorgeous images found here. Pat Hayward and David Winger took on the daunting task of photo selection and editing.

Finally, words cannot express enough gratitude for the individuals at Denver Botanic Gardens, Colorado State University, and private businesses who individually and collectively provide the support and expertise to make Plant Select one of the country's most progressive and innovative plant programs.

PHOTO CREDITS

Bill Adams, pages 30, 74, 92, 120, and 127.

Jason Baker, page 223.

Randy Baldwin, page 160.

Lisa Bird, page 81.

Michael Bone, pages 80, 166, and 188.

Lisa Brown, page 39.

Betty Cahill, pages 212 and 213.

Brooke Colburn, page 142.

CSU Extension Master Gardeners of Broomfield, page 46.

Gary Epstein, pages 177 and 222.

Nate Fetig, page 189.

Kirk Fieseler, pages 27, 28, 31, 33, and 35.

Margaret Foderaro, page 193.

Greg Foreman, pages 6–7, 67, 77, 93, 105, 156, 186, and 224.

Kelly Grummons, page 42.

Pat Hayward, pages 2, 9, 12, 15, 23, 24, 25, 26, 29, 32, 34, 36, 44, 50, 52, 56, 57, 59, 60, 63, 64, 72, 73, 75, 82, 83, 84, 85, 87, 88, 89, 94, 97, 100, 101, 104, 106, 108, 109, 110, 114, 116, 122, 124, 126, 129, 132, 136, 143, 144, 146, 148, 150, 151, 154, 155, 175, 176, 178, 182, 185, 190, 194, 195, 198, 204, 208, 209 top, 210, 211, 221, and 244.

Shalene Hiller, page 10.

Mervi Hjelmroos-Koski, page 206.

Dan Johnson, pages 4–5, 152, and 153.

Panayoti Kelaidis, pages 37, 38, 62, 65, 68, 76, 102, 103, 107, 111, 112, 115, 125, 139, 163, 205, and 218.

Mike Kintgen, page 91.

North Creek Nurseries, pages 164 and 165.

Diana Reavis, pages 22, 71, 134, and 191.

David Salman, pages 45, 66, and 158.

Judy Sedbrook, pages 19, 113, and 174.

Scott Skogerboe, pages 157 and 207 bottom.

David Staats, pages 20, 21, 40, 78, 98, 99, and 172.

Carla Tews, pages 69, 70, 169, 170, and 171.

Alan Tower, page 43.

Keith Williamson, pages 49 and 121.

Diane Wilson, page 90.

David Winger, pages 16, 17, 18, 41, 47, 48, 51, 53, 54, 55, 58, 61, 79, 86, 95, 96, 117, 119, 123, 128, 130, 131, 133, 135, 137, 138, 140, 141, 145, 147, 149, 159, 160, 167, 168, 173, 179, 181, 183, 184, 187, 192, 196, 197, 199, 200, 201, 202, 203, 207 top, 209 bottom, 214, 215, 216, 217, 219, 220, and 242.

INDEX

Bold-faced page numbers indicate main entries.

ABOUT THE AUTHOR

PLANT SELECT is a nonprofit collaboration of Colorado State University, Denver Botanic Gardens, and professional horticulturists whose goal is to find, test, and distribute plants designed to thrive in the high plains and intermountain region, and anywhere that water resources are of concern. Driven by the belief that the right plants in the right place matter and that tougher growing environments require smarter approaches, Plant Select leverages a uniquely collaborative model and highly selective cultivation process to identify plants that thrive on less water and provide gardeners with smart, stunning, and successful gardens using fewer resources and with less environmental impact.

Page 2: Yellow-flowered *Chrysothamnus nauseosus* (baby blue rabbitbrush) mingles with grasses in the harsh plains flanking the Rocky Mountains.

Pages 4–5: *Agastache rupestris* (sunset hyssop).

Copyright ©2017 by Plant Select®. All rights reserved.
Photo and illustration credits appear on page 245.

Published in 2017 by Timber Press, Inc.

The Haseltine Building
133 S.W. Second Avenue, Suite 450
Portland, Oregon 97204-3527
timberpress.com

Printed in China

Cover design by Kristi Pfeffer
Text design by Laura Shaw Design, Inc.

ISBN 13: 978-1-60469-735-3

Catalog records for this book are available from the Library of Congress and the British Library.